THE BAYSWATER

Brasserie
BOOK OF FOOD

THE BAYSWATER

Brasserie

BOOK OF FOOD

TONY PAPAS   HAMISH KEITH

Photographs by
ROBIN MORRISON

Ten Speed Press
Berkeley, California

ACKNOWLEDGEMENTS

This book was made possible with the help of Willy Wild who heads our kitchen team, Christopher Walton, our pastry chef who creates the Bayswater Brasserie's desserts and pastries, and Carmel Caridade and the rest of the kitchen staff who have helped develop these recipes. I would also like to mention the team at Simon and Schuster, particularly my publisher, Kirsty Melville, photographer Robin Morrison, designer Susan Kinealy, Laurine Croasdale, who knocked the text into its final shape, and editor Susan Morris-Yates.

THE BAYSWATER BRASSERIE BOOK OF FOOD

First published in Australia in 1989 by
Simon & Schuster Australia
7 Grosvenor Place, Brookvale NSW 2100

©1989 by Hamish Keith and Tony Papas

TEN SPEED PRESS
P.O. Box 7123
Berkeley, California 94707

Cover Design by Fifth Street Associates
Book Design by Susan Kinealy
Typeset in Australia by Midland Typesetters

ISBN 0-89815-367-0

Library of Congress Cataloging-in-Publication Data

Papas, Tony.

The Bayswater Brasserie book of food / Tony Papas, Hamish Keith: photography by Robin Morrison.
p. cm.

"First published in Australia in 1989 by Simon & Schuster Australia . . . Brookvale, NSW" — T.p. verso.

ISBN 0-89815-367-0: $24.95

1. Cookery, Australian. 2. Bayswater Brasserie (Sydney, N.S.W.)
I. Keith, Hamish, 1936– . II. Bayswater Brasserie (Sydney, N.S.W.) III. Title.

TX725.A9P26 1989
641.5'09944'1–dc20   89-20623
                                                    CIP

Printed in Singapore by Toppan Printing Co. Pty Ltd

Contents

INTRODUCTION FOR AMERICAN READERS

The Bayswater Brasserie Book of Food is a book about informal eating and cooking — the ingredients, freshness and quality being of utmost importance. Some of the fruits, vegetables and seafoods are indigenous to this part of the world. It also deals with some new methods of cookery which we developed here at the Bayswater Brasserie.

We have mentioned a number of new ingredients frequently used at the Bayswater Brasserie, however we have refrained from using rarefied or obscure ingredients.

Another aim of the book was to write recipes which are easy to follow and would enable the reader to visualise the dish they were about to cook. Healthier food, less affected by long-winded unnecessary preparation, is much more appropriate to our way of life.

The Bayswater Brasserie serves food all day long and has an extensive menu so that the diner can design his or her meal to suit his or her particular needs.

The book carries recipes from Breakfast through Supper and includes dishes which might be termed as 'comfort food', such as Porridge with Black Sugar and Ginger. Other lively combinations are Poached Eggs in Salads, four different methods of marinating fish (served with an old fashioned type of hearth bread), Fresh Saffron Noodles with Cured Ocean Trout and Olive Puree, and BBQ Baby Octopus with suggested accompaniments.

There are many similarities between Australia and the United States in terms of our food and cooking. We share a healthy approach to our cooking — we are not inhibited to borrow from the cuisines of other nations. This has happened for two reasons. People are better traveled than they were 30 years ago and various ethnic groups have settled here and in the United States, contributing to the available ingredients and styles of cooking.

We are experiencing in Australia a similar renaissance to what has been experienced in the United States. For example, Australia now produces many cheeses which can hold their own against the cheeses of France and Italy. As in the United States, organically grown vegetables, sun-ripened fruits and vegetables, and a move toward solving the inherent problems of sustainable agriculture in an effort to look after our health and environment, are all at the top of the list of priorities.

The move toward less complicated, fresher Brasserie-style food is an important trend. Unlike trends which have gone before us, this one is here to stay and will become the first real step toward the development of a cuisine of our own.

It is here to stay because we are not just copying another style of food, like the French provincial cooking in the 70s. We are now developing our own style using influences from other food cultures. The other development has been the communication between consumers and producers. Restaurants are largely responsible for a new and better produce served on people's plates. As this collaboration with restaurants and producers continues, regional food will begin to appear and eventually a cuisine will emerge.

The Bayswater Brasserie is a very important cog in this movement because of the number of people it feeds. Unlike many large establishments, the food is prepared and served with care, enthusiasm, and creativity. The kitchen responds quickly to new ingredients and is committed to serving food of consistently high standards in terms of taste and presentation. The combinations are both simple and spontaneous.

Introduction

My daily fare may have been pretty standard New Zealand for the time, enlivened by a greater variety of seafood perhaps, but at my grandparents' house across town in Ponsonby, things were a bit different. My grandfather was Greek and one of my uncles had travelled extensively in Europe and in Greece. There we ate exotic things like stuffed eggplant and vegetables one did not usually encounter on New Zealand tables a generation ago, red capsicum and zucchini for instance. My grandmother was Scottish and she had a wonderful repertoire of hearty puddings and stews and things like whole baked fish stuffed with zucchini. Remembering those particular delights has made me reflect more and more on the fact that cuisine has something to do with what a person is and not just what recipes they can follow.

My father was in charge of seafood in our house. One great adventure was the occasional sack of crayfish, mussels, paua (our New Zealand name for abalone), cockles, the giant bivalve toeroa, now a forbidden dish, or pippies that our Maori neighbours would give us. Those sacks had an unforgettable damp smell of salt and seaweed. In their gift too were great newspaper parcels of snapper, kawhai, cod or kingfish.

Those cooking smells of our parents' and grandparents' kitchens are a good reminder of what skills our ancestor cooks had to master in their cooking. No thermostats, fan-forced ovens or meat thermometers then, just a good and well trained nose for the right smells of baking meat, browning pastry or rising dough. They are, or ought to be, part of our cooking skills today. Our nose and eyes can tell us a great deal more than the dials on our space age ovens ever could.

Up until after World War II the popular diet in New Zealand and Australia remained the debased, colonial version of working-class English cooking. Heaps of meat and overcooked vegetables. The English writer, Eric Linklater, on a visit to New Zealand and Australia in 1952, described the Antipodean method of cooking roast mutton as being something akin to blowing a sheep up with a hand grenade, the fragments being burnt in the resulting fire. Prophetically, he also wondered what a French country housewife would do if given the wonderful ingre'.....ts available to our Southern cooks. Linklater would hardly recognise cooking in this part of the world now. A variety of post war influences have transformed it. Not the least of these being the very French provincial cuisine he so unfavourably compared it with.

When the brasserie style of restaurant arrived in Sydney in the early eighties, it could have easily been dismissed as simply another fashionable variation on a theme. The high cuisine of classical French and French provincial cooking will no doubt always have their niche in the Australian culinary scheme of things. Australia's ethnic restaurants, Asian or European, will endure too and gain in strength as the cultures they represent make their continuing impact on modern Australian life. But other styles have come and gone as fleeting and hardly any more enduring than the fashions in restaurant interiors.

There were plenty of food writers and foodies prepared to predict that the bloom of brasseries would go the same way. Certainly, where the style was more in the dress of the floor staff than in any essential philosophy of the kitchen, that prediction was true.

The original French brasserie only incidentally served food. Traditionally they were places in the eastern parts of France where beer and cider were made and served along with some pretty basic fare—charcuterie and choucroute with garnishes of boiled potatoes and smoked pork, mustard and, of course, the ubiquitous French bread. These simple establishments were transformed by the Parisians into the wonderful cafes we know them as today. But as amazingly varied as their contemporary menus are, there is an essential simplicity to their dishes which marks the style as innovative and versatile.

It is no accident that the brasserie arrived on the Australian scene when the idea of an Australian cuisine was being widely, if self-consciously, discussed. Those discussions were not isolated from those about other facets of an Australian identity or Australian achievement. The reality of such a notion may not matter much. Ironically, an Australian cuisine will have arrived when discussing it is no longer necessary, when an approach to food and its preparation is as naturally and unselfconsciously Australian as two-up on ANZAC Day.

Perhaps more than any other approach to public food, the brasserie kitchen offers a scope for easy innovation, a quick response to new ingredients. The brasserie kitchen readily accomodates change and as a restaurant ambience it attracts a clientele whose demanding participation in shaping the style is one of its strengths.

It was this basic philosophy which appealed to myself and my two partners, Dean Williams and Robert Smallbone, and formed the basis for our research and transformation of two old terrace buildings on Bayswater Road, Kings Cross into the present Brasserie. We set out to build an elegant cafe which embodied the atmosphere of brasseries and cafes we had seen throughout Europe—the hard surfaces and straightforward materials and the congenial, informal atmosphere— all suggested a style of restaurant that would easily translate to the style of life evolving here. The building had to have several different dining areas, such as the garden or conservatory overlooking the street, yet have a grand feeling of space. A stimulating, but easy atmosphere where friends greet each other from table to table, where even the lone diner feels comfortably a part of it all, and where the meals of the day imperceptibly merge without rigid timetables.

The atmosphere of Bayswater Brasserie also suits the Australian style. The bustle and chatter, the waiters and busboys speeding around, the energy flowing from the kitchen out into the public space, the clatter of forks and dishes, the

Introduction

hard surfaces softened with lush plants or enriched with bold colours, the displays of pastries and tempting desserts, the rows of preserves and pickles, the piles of magazines and newspapers.

Fresh ingredients and seasons of the year are the only limits to the Bayswater menu. In addition to the permanent menu there is a blackboard of daily specials which allows for a great variety of dishes according to market produce. This flexibility has enabled me to draw on a wide range of influences and ideas from my childhood as well as more recent experiences from travelling and living overseas. The simplicity of dishes and preference for hearty fare suits the informal dining style at the Brasserie and allows diners to mould and develop our menu according to their appetite. And perhaps as importantly, the brasserie style is one which can remain richly exciting while satisfying our concerns for a healthier diet.

In the seven years it has been open the Bayswater Brasserie has evolved into something singularly its own. The range and style of its dishes has grown, for instance, and its continuing success relies not only on the commitment and skills of the three original partners, but on a talented staff of sixty.

Tony Papas
Sydney
1989

The Cook and the Kitchen

It might seem an odd thing to begin with, but what we would look for in the well managed kitchen, or if not exactly in the kitchen, in easy reach of the cook, would be book shelves and well stocked book shelves at that. Beginner or expert, no cook can do without books. Not just recipe books, although we all need plenty of those, but all kinds of books on food and cuisines, and the people committed to and inventing both.

The cook's imagination needs to be well fed and the literature on food is immense. For something like two millennia Europeans have been writing on food and recording discoveries about the chemistry of the kitchen. Travellers, adventurers and explorers have been defining newly encountered cultures by what they eat and how they cook, and bringing back marvellous new things to their own kitchens.

In the history of European imperialism the ingredients for Dutch, Portuguese, Spanish and English kitchens have played an enormous part. Even in our own time two European countries have almost come to the brink of a hot war over the humble cod. Armies, according to Napoleon, march on their stomachs, and it is equally a fact that on more than a few occasions armies have marched and fleets set sail all in the cause of their national pantries.

Little wonder then that writing about food is a branch of literature in its own right. The sensible cook will mine that amazing resource for all they are worth, and garner from it the insights, techniques and inspirations that mark the good cook from the plain preparer of food. The more the cook can devour from the literature of food, the more their guests will be delighted with their creations.

The cuisine of the Bayswater Brasserie is eclectic and is therefore an excellent reflection and focus for the evolving cuisine of Australia and New Zealand. We can call on any technique we choose, any kind of cuisine or combination of ingredients that takes our fancy, and we are only limited by our imagination and what the fish, meat and vegetable markets have fresh on offer.

We can also be limited by our kitchens.

It is true that amazing meals can be constructed on a sheet of red-hot iron or on an arrangement of old kerosene tins. Unforgettable meals can emerge from tiny cabins on yachts or the ashes of a campfire in the bush. But in the normal order of things the committed cook would prefer a well organised and well stocked kitchen in which to manage their culinary feats.

Probably the primary requirement of the good kitchen is plenty of light and plenty of space. If the daytime light that floods the bench comes from a garden aspect, so much the better. A good kitchen ought to provoke a sense of contentment and creativity by its ambience alone.

If you are starting from scratch, just bear in mind that cooks know more about kitchens than architects, builders or plumbers. And you will know better than anyone just exactly how your cooking routine is arranged. Physically your kitchen, in the ideal world, will be a reflection of your own methods of cooking.

For most people those methods are instinctive and usually adapted to an existing kitchen layout and space. If you are designing a new kitchen, take some time to carefully analyse how you work and, in particular, how many of those methods are habits forced on you by an existing kitchen and which you would like changed in the new.

Walk through, in your mind, the whole process from coming home with the fresh ingredients and storing them away in refrigerator, dry store or pantry to plating up the finished dish for serving. Many cooks work most efficiently in a kind of circle or triangle built around stove, refrigerator and other immediate storage spaces for utensils and ingredients, and sinks linked by bench spaces with different functions.

The worst possible model is the all too common straight line of bench, sink, stove and refrigerator. Think of the cook's kitchen space as being like a cockpit in the centre of operations, with all the major equipment easily in reach. Think too of how much easier cooking is if the accumulating clutter is reduced to a minimum, so pans, sinks and dishwashers have a place in this central layout too. Two sinks are better than one and, if you have the space, three is probably the ideal number.

The principal bench space will obviously be for preparation and the next most important will be for assembling what the French call the *mise en place*— all the ingredients, prepared and assembled in the order you will need them during cooking. Obviously time limitations will mean that some preparation will have to go on during cooking, but as an ideal it is a good habit to finish it all before any cooking starts—there is no worse cooking panic than a frantic hunt for a spice or whatever while a pan on the stove is about to catch or explode.

Storage of utensils is another matter of personal preference but do not rule out installing large bin-like drawers for your pans; they have a great many advantages over shelves and cupboards for such things.

Dry goods need a good accessible storage area; a walk-in pantry is ideal, or cupboards with shallow shelves. Things like spices need to be stored in easy reach of the stove and preparation bench. Dry goods like pasta and flours can be further away.

If you are stuck with somebody else's idea of a kitchen, then carefully plan how to utilise that space to your own best advantage and, as part of your meal plan, also anticipate how the preparation of that particular menu will be organised.

STOVES, OVENS AND HOBS

The first decision to make is about the fuel your kitchen will employ. Gas has some obvious advantages over electricity, such as instant control over the amount of heat on the bottom of the pan. But gas also needs a good and constant pressure and without the right plumbing this is sometimes difficult to achieve. Check with the supplier and with your neighbours about the gas pressure in your part of the street—it is not always a constant.

Small commercial gas ovens and stove tops are preferable to the usual domestic models. There is generally more room on top and they are capable of delivering greater pressure and thus more heat than standard gas stoves. Obviously, they are not as pretty as the designer kitchen range, but prettiness takes a pretty low second place to efficiency when you are looking for what is, after all, the engine room of your kitchen.

The commercial designs also often allow for a greater variety of cooking techniques. Some have a built-in barbecue or char-griller and griddle plates and they also allow for using a wok on the hobs—something a lot of domestic designs cannot accommodate. Make sure the barbecue can deliver enough heat—many domestic designs and some commercial ones do not—and keep in mind that with the degree of heat these kinds of stoves can deliver you will almost certainly need exhaust fan ventilation in the kitchen. Some kind of ventilation in any kitchen, especially if you have a living area nearby, is a good idea.

If you are restricted to domestic designs a combination of gas hobs and electric oven can be reasonably efficient. Fan-forced electric ovens distribute an even heat and are very efficient. They are therefore often hotter than the conventional oven design so you may need to set your thermostat 40°C (100°F) lower.

In any case, the efficiency of most oven thermostats is reasonably relative, so getting to know your own oven by sight and smell, as well as reading the dials, is an essential. The nose is one of the cook's best instruments and it can very efficiently detect the difference between cooking, burning and not cooking at all—the right heat smells right.

At the risk of seeming like some Luddite of the kitchen, the only use we can think of for microwave ovens is for reheating takeaways. It is a sad reflection though on marketing efficiency, if not of these ovens, that even in the tinier bars of Barcelona nowadays the tapas go into the microwave before being served.

KNIVES AND OTHER THINGS

The well managed kitchen cannot have too many knives, nor can they be too sharp. These are the cook's basic tools and a blunt knife is more dangerous than a sharp one. You can make do with four basic knives.

- A 25 cm (10 in) chef's knife for chopping and slicing.
- A 15 cm (6 in) chef's knife, sometimes called an office knife, for general purposes.
- A thin-bladed boning knife for fish and meat.
- A paring or turning knife for splitting, peeling or cutting batons from vegetables.

A sharp vegetable peeler is also an essential and the chain store variety with a scooped and slotted blade hung in a plastic bow is one of the better kinds.

Handling knives is one of the first kitchen techniques to master. Properly cut, sliced, diced or chopped ingredients make an enormous difference to the quality and texture of the dish. Some cooks argue that it also makes a detectable difference to flavour as well.

It is a good idea to have your knives professionally sharpened at least once a year. In between, you should have a steel or bench stone to keep their edge. Do not put your knives in the dishwasher, the heat dulls their edge and temper, and destroys the texture of their handles if you have had the good taste to choose wooden handled knives.

With good knives you will also need a good chopping board. We prefer wooden boards, but they need regular attention such as salting and scrubbing to keep them sweet. New Zealand kauri wood boards are among the best, but that wood is now a prohibited export so they are hard to come by. New Guinea kauri is a reasonable second choice. Beech makes an excellent board, some cooks say the best, and pine will do, although this wood has a short life in the kitchen. Some cooks soak their chopping boards in a good olive oil—an expensive habit, but one that helps keep the board reasonably impervious to flavours and meat juices.

Regardless of the wood, the boards should be absolutely flat—for safety as well as efficiency—and when they begin to be bowed from use or if they warp, either have them planed flat or get a new one. After washing and oiling, store them on edge with plenty of air around them otherwise they are likely to become a home for bacteria.

For the recipes in this book other essential tools: are a good rolling pin and a cool rolling slab (it is not a bad idea to have part of your bench surface of wood for this), tongs, wire whisk, ladle, steel spatula, slotted spoon, large sieve, strainer, colander for draining and refreshing, blanching basket, fish slice, mortar and pestle, zester, and a good array of wooden spoons and spatulas.

You will also need a good variety of stainless steel or crockery mixing bowls, a good measuring jug, scales, a number of shallow bowls, and plates for assembling prepared ingredients.

Kitchen machinery should include a food mill, a food processor and a pasta machine. Dried pasta is a fine and useful basic, but to make some of the noodle dishes in this book you will need to make your own fresh.

Pots and pans are a matter of choice. Your preference for a cooking style will have a lot to do with what lurks in your pan drawers and what is constantly on top of the stove or in the oven. For brasserie style cooking you will need a few ordinary black steel frying or saute pans of various sizes. These should be cured in the method given on page 37 in the omelette recipe. They need a lot of care and should almost never be washed, but scoured with salt and lightly oiled after use.

You will need a variety of good heavy-based saucepans and pots. The most useful we can suggest for the domestic kitchen are stainless steel with heavy and thick cast copper or aluminium plate bottoms. They are not as good a heat conducter as the all-aluminium or copper pot , but they are the easiest to clean and handle. Obviously the specialist kitchen will also have a store of copper, iron and aluminium pots for different uses. Egg whites and sugars, for example, are thought to behave best in copper. Some big 4, 6 and 8 L (7, 10 and 14 pt) stock pots are also essential. When using aluminium pots never stir with anything but a wooden spoon, as it may discolour or taint the flavour of the ingredients.

Some of the ingredients in the book need deep frying so at the very least you should equip yourself with a deep-frying basket and a thermometer. For risotto, indulge yourself with a high-sided iron pot, enamelled inside.

For the oven, heavy iron or ceramic ware is best. Choose something that will diffuse the heat evenly and something attractive enough to serve from to save double handling of hot dishes and washing up.

You will need a good wok and some bamboo steamers to use in conjunction with it. Buy the wok from Chinese shops rather than the expensive teflon-lined models you are likely to be offered in department stores or kitchen shops. In fact, as a general rule, stores that cater for professional cooks or particular cuisines would be more suitable than glossy designer kitchen shops. It is not a bad idea to do some serious reading on traditional utensils before equipping a kitchen and writers like Elizabeth David are an excellent guide to these.

Utensils have evolved out of methods over a long period of trial and error, and a pot or pan designed for a particular purpose, such as poaching, or cooking an omelette, did not get that way by chance. A good kitchen rule is that the right pot for the job is the right pot for the job!

In addition, you will need cake tins, bread tins and a good variety of moulds for a variety of dishes. Second-hand shops are often a good source of these and the traditionally shaped Victorian jelly moulds should be seized when seen.

Heavy baking and roasting trays are another essential. They should be treated in much the same way as your frying pans, just wiped and oiled, but not washed. The best are kicked up at the edges to prevent twisting in the hot oven and to hold any spills. They improve with age.

COOKING METHODS AND TERMS

Like the names for food, there is a considerable variation from cuisine to cuisine about cooking terms. These are what we mean by them in this book and are by no means intended to be a definitive list.

BASTING
To moisten food while it is roasting, either with its own fat or juices or some additional liquid prepared for that purpose.

BARBECUE OR CHAR-GRILL
Smaller cuts of meat or fish and some vegetables are seared or sealed on top of an extremely hot grill and moved to a slightly cooler spot to complete cooking. The method should mark the food with a typical criss-cross pattern. Only enough oil is used to prevent the meat or fish sticking to the bars of the grill—too much will burn and leave a smoky flavour.

BEATING
A vigorous mixing or whacking together of tougher ingredients. Use a whisk, egg-beater, or blender or food processor.

BLENDING
To mix food less vigorously than beating using a pastry scraper or wooden spoon.

BLANCH
To plunge ingredients into boiling water, which is usually then returned to the boil. Meat is usually blanched to remove excess salt, some superficial fat or to remove any dirt and rubbish. Vegetables are generally refreshed in iced or cold running water immediately after they have been blanched.

BRAISING
Slow roasting in the oven with liquid, and usually covered. This method is used for tougher cuts of meat or for pieces like shanks where cartilage needs to be converted to collagen. The food is sometimes coloured on top of the stove before braising, and can be marinated for some time before cooking in the final liquid.

BIND
To hold together using a binding agent such as choux pastry, breadcrumbs or egg whites.

CHOP AND DICE
Food cut into small pieces which we specify as either fine or rough. The French, who make a science of these matters, have names for the various grades of chopping or dicing. Dicing is most often applied to longer, round vegetables like carrots or celery, or when something like an onion or turnip is intended to be cut through into round slices rather than chopped into fragments.

Deep frying

To deep fry successfully needs the right oil and the right heat—grape seed oil is expensive but the best, sunflower oil will do very well and some things, like small fish, are best done in olive oil, but be careful since this has a relatively low smoke point. A thermometer is essential, as olive oil needs to be a constant 160°C (325°F) and other oils 10°C (50°F) higher. To keep a constant heat, only small batches of ingredients should go into the hot oil at once, so as to keep plenty of space between the food pieces.

Deglazing

To rinse the left over juices from a roasting or saute pan or saucepan with some liquid like white wine or vinegar or even plain water, thus making a reduction for a sauce. Deglazing with vinegar, for instance, will convert any fat into something safer and more useful to the flavour. Sometimes the pan is deglazed until absolutely dry, but the residue will still combine with and colour the following sauce ingredients that go into it.

Fold

The blending together of more fragile ingredients, like egg whites into a souffle base or cream into the already mixed custard. The term really describes the action, which is always carried out with a wooden spatula or flat wooden spoon, except for egg whites which are sometimes better handled with a steel spoon.

Gratine

To brown a dish under a grill or salamander. Traditionally this latter was a heavy steel plate on a handle, heated until red hot, then held closely over the top of the dish that needs the tan. The food is normally sauced first or covered with breadcrumbs, cheese or knobs of butter to form a crust. Care is required not to turn a good dish into a shrivelled disaster.

Grilling

The Americans call this broiling. This is the method of completely cooking a dish under the grill; and the same caution about overcooking should be exercised.

Pan frying or sauteeing

Oil or butter is heated, without the oil smoking or the butter burning, in a flattish pan to quickly cook small cuts of meat, fish, fritters, pancakes or blanched vegetables. The cooking residues are often deglazed and used as the basis of a sauce. This is a quick, versatile and controllable cooking method and the one most employed in the brasserie kitchen. Oil and butter combined is a common medium for the method. The oil is heated first and then the butter is dropped in.

Poaching

Fish, meat and eggs are cooked in a simmering liquid—stock, plain water and sometimes milk. This is a slow and gentle method of cooking and the liquid, often seasoned with various herbs, should barely move during the process.

POT ROASTING

Meat browned on top of the stove, then cooked in the oven in a heavy casserole or pot covered with a lid. Butter is often used as the medium and root vegetables can be combined with cuts of meat. The method gives a constant moist heat but not as moist as braising. With a good heat and a heavy sealed pot, this method can sometimes be used on the stove top if your oven is full. The roasting meat should fit fairly tightly in the pot.

PUREE

To reduce solid foods alone, or in combination, to a consistent paste. This can be done in a mortar with a pestle, with a sieve and wooden mushroom, a mouli or food mill, a mincer or food processor. Different foods will require a different machine and we indicate the one or combination we think best in each recipe.

REDUCE

Boiling down a liquid, like a stock or sauce, to reduce it in volume and concentrate its elements into stronger flavour or colour.

REFRESH

The second stage in the blanching process. After briefly cooking the food, it is plunged into icy or cold water to halt the cooking process. Some cooks argue that pasta needs this treatment while others argue to the contrary. Boiled eggs certainly do.

ROASTING

Cooking meat or vegetables in an open pan in a hot oven. Meat should be sealed on top of the stove before roasting, and meat and vegetables should be constantly basted during cooking. Anything roasted needs to rest in a warm place, the oven for instance, before carving or serving to let the juices in the meat settle down and disperse evenly throughout.

SKIM

To remove the fats, grease or scum from stocks, sauces, jams and poached fruits while they cook.This is best done with a ladle or a skimmer—a long-handled flattish perforated spoon, sometimes of fine mesh.

STIR FRY

Small pieces of food—meat or vegetables—cooked in a wok or pan on a high heat while constantly being moved during cooking. Clarified butter or oil is the medium, sometimes combined with a little stock, citrus juice or wine during the process. In a wok the food is constantly pulled up from the centre to the cooler sides.

TOASTING

The browning of breadcrumbs, slices of bread, pancetta or similar meats, ground spices or polenta, on a flat tray under a grill.

STOCKING THE KITCHEN

The well managed kitchen should always be able to provide a delicious, if simple, lunch. As a test of your own resources see what your kitchen could produce at a moment's notice, and if the product is dull or cannot be done, you do not have a well stocked kitchen.

When deciding on your menu always try to keep in mind seasonal ingredients. It is possible to get most things most times of the year, but there is a pleasant relationship between the dishes we eat and the seasons we eat them. A seasonal pattern to menus makes sense and it is something that informs the variations of menu at the Bayswater Brasserie.

There is a lot of romantic nonsense associated with the idea of European peasant food. Up until at least the late eighteenth century, when the French Revolution and the ideas it exported elsewhere in Europe opened up the wild larder to ordinary people, it was probably pretty ordinary stuff based on porridges and grains with little meat. But one idea is probably true, that the country diet was seasonal and the inventive cook made the most of what was fresh and available as a relief from stored grains or root vegetables. It is a pattern well worth following in our very different lifestyle.

Most of the dishes in this book use some ingredients essential to the basic kitchen supplies. Stocks, of course, are the king and queen of all of these. They take time to make, and a good stock needs more than a little nursing as it goes. However, they are easy to store in the freezer in small quantities, and are an amazing consumer of leftover meat, poultry and vegetable scraps.

The well managed kitchen should never be without a good supply of fresh and dried herbs and spices. If at all possible establish a small kitchen garden of at least basil, thyme, parsley and mint. On a more ambitious scale you could grow rosemary, sage and, perhaps, a small bay tree. All of these can be grown in pots.

All herbs and spices, dried or not, need to be reasonably fresh. They will not keep for very long once they have been opened so keep your stocks of them small and well managed.

Also stock some liquid ingredients such as a good cooking sherry, balsamic vinegar, mirin (a clear Japanese rice wine), and, of course, the best extra virgin olive oil you can find. There are many brands of extra virgin olive oil and they all have their fierce proponents. Most non-partisan cooks, though, agree that Colonna, from Molise in central Italy, is one of the best.

There is a bit of a cottage industry in writing books about herbs and spices and other kitchen ingredients, and not all of the works in the canon are particularly reliable. Many of them reflect national confusions about the proper names for things and, without wanting to pick on the Americans, a lot of US ingredient books are not particularly helpful in this part of the world.

Poached Eggs on Salad Leaves with Smoked Ocean Trout   See page 38

Black Pudding with Sauteed Apples and Fried Mashed Potato   See page 43

One marvellous exception is the encyclopaedia *Food* by Waverley Root. This is an exhaustive guide that nobody interested in food should be without. Equally useful is the new and revised *Larousse Gastronomique*. The original and earlier editions were remarkably chauvinist, admitting to very little outside the borders of France. The new version is truly international and extremely helpful.

One classic book on basic ingredients is Elizabeth David's *Spices, Salt and Aromatics in the English Kitchen*. In fact, with the possible exception of her work on Italian food, all of Elizabeth David's books should be on the kitchen shelf. Another useful book on kitchen ingredients is *Herbs, Spices and Flavourings* by Tom Stobart.

Finally, and not the least important of kitchen stocks, is a good supply of dried pasta. Whole books have been written on the subject of this fascinating invention and despite the persistent myth that Marco Polo brought it back from China, credit for its invention must go to the Italians. Dried pasta is recorded there, as a valuable item in someone's estate, a generation before that intrepid explorer set out on his travels.

There is plenty of dried pasta available and a great deal of it is not worth cooking. Make sure what you buy is made from the hard-grain durum wheat flour and not the softer farina. It should look yellowish not grey, and should list fresh eggs among its ingredients, with superior brands specifying a slow drying process. The pasta should have been rolled or pushed through bronze dies to ensure that it has a rough porous surface for better sauce absorption. It should not look smooth textured.

The very best brand of dried pasta exported from Italy is Martelli and that should set a standard against which you can judge other brands, local or Italian. It is made in a small family factory in Tuscany and is sold in distinctive bright yellow packets with printed handwritten instructions.

Kitchen Basics

If you are stuck for stock you can buy commercial bouillons and consommes, but this ought to be the good cook's very last resort. Get into a pattern of setting aside some time every few months for making stock. The recipes given here have been developed with the home kitchen in mind using whole ingredients rather than trimmings. Consequently they have a full-bodied flavour and can be diluted.

Stocks are always unsalted and seldom spiced with anything but pepper. Some stocks, such as lamb, might be flavoured with garlic and the occasional fresh herb like rosemary, but as a basic rule stocks are the foundation ingredient of many dishes and need to be left as versatile to flavour as possible.

Stocks must be skimmed throughout, they should never be left with a layer of grease, fat or scum on top. Always endeavour to keep the stock clear, which is why they are never cooked covered. A lid will simply catch the scum carried by the steam and drop it back into the pot. A simple way to make skimming easier is to top up the liquid with cold water. This will slightly harden the fats and make them easier to lift.

Meat or chicken stocks can be white or brown. The colour is provided by browning any bone first and adding the deglazed pan juices to the basic stock liquid. Add water throughout cooking to help maintain the level of liquid in the stock.

VEAL STOCK
TO MAKE 5 L (8 pts)

2 kg (4½ lb) veal shanks
2 kg (4½ lb) veal bones
4 medium onions, peeled and halved
olive oil
6 sticks celery, topped
3 large leeks

4 medium carrots
1 teaspoon black peppercorns
2 fresh bay leaves
10 tomatoes
12 large mushrooms
½ bunch parsley stalks (keep the leaves for something else)
2 sprigs of thyme

Thoroughly brown the shanks and bones in a hot oven 200°C (400°F). Blacken the onions in a cast iron pan or on a hot plate. Brown the rest of the vegetables in a little olive oil. Put all the ingredients in a large stock pot and cover with 6 L (10 pts) cold water, bring to the boil and simmer for 6–8 hours, skimming regularly. Carefully strain into suitable containers to store.

CHICKEN STOCK

TO MAKE 5 L (8 pts)

2 large boiling chickens
1.5 kg (3 lb 5oz) chicken bones
6 sticks celery, topped
3 large leeks
3 medium onions, whole and peeled

3 medium carrots, whole and peeled
2 bay leaves
½ teaspoon black peppercorns
2 sprigs of thyme

Remove any visible fat from the chickens. Wash them and the bones thoroughly in cold water. Put them in a large stock pot covered with 6 L (10 pts) cold water and bring to the boil without the other ingredients. Skim thoroughly, add the vegetables and simmer for 3–4 hours, skimming regularly and keeping the level of the liquid maintained. Strain and store.

To make brown chicken stock, brown the ingredients as for the veal stock. To make a duck stock use exactly the same method using duck carcasses and legs instead of the whole bird.

CHICKEN CONSOMME

Consomme is a clarified stock.

TO MAKE 2 L (3½ pts)

250 g (9 oz) lean chicken or veal meat
1 medium onion, peeled and roughly chopped
1 medium carrot, peeled and roughly chopped
1 large leek, split and roughly chopped
1 stick celery, roughly chopped

½ bunch parsley stalks
2 tablespoons salt
1 teaspoon black pepper
4 egg whites
2½ litres (4½ pts) Chicken Stock (see page 23)

Remove any fat from the meat. Mix the meat and vegetables together and push through the medium grill of a mincer. Season, add the egg whites, and mix thoroughly. Put in a small stock pot and add the cold chicken stock, mixing thoroughly. Bring slowly to the boil, stirring all the time. As it begins to boil and the clarification starts to set, stop stirring and reduce the heat. Simmer, allowing the stock to bubble gently for a further 45 minutes. When cooked remove gently from the heat. Through a hole in the clarification ladle the soup into a strainer lined with a tea towel or muslin cloth into a clean pot.

FISH STOCK

TO MAKE 5 L (8 pts)

1.5 kg (3 lb 5 oz) flathead heads, gills and
  guts removed
1.5 kg (3 lb 5 oz) white fish bones
100 g (4 oz) butter
3 large leeks, sliced

2 medium onions, sliced
2 large fennel bulbs, sliced
2 fresh bay leaves
juice of 1 lemon
1 bunch parsley stalks

Chop the fish and bones into manageable bits.

Heat the butter in the small stock pot and saute all the ingredients except the bay leaves, the juice and the parsley stalks. Saute without colouring for 4–5 minutes. Cover with 5 L (8 pts) cold water, add the bay leaves and lemon juice, and bring to the boil. Skim well and simmer for 10 minutes. Add the parsley and simmer for a further 10 minutes. Strain and store.

BREADS

F ew domestic ovens will get up enough heat to cook pizza and fougasse breads. If you can supply enough heat, you can improve the effectiveness of your steel oven by adding a ceramic kiln tile to its interior furniture. This should be about 2 cm (¾ in) smaller all around than the rack it sits on to allow good heat circulation. It will never be quite as good as the traditional brick bread oven but it will make an enormous improvement to the quality of the heat you need for bread baking.

The breads, particularly pizza and fougasse, can be baked sitting directly on the ceramic tile.

COUNTRY BREAD

FOR THE MOTHER DOUGH:

25 g (1 oz) fresh yeast
150 ml (5 fl oz) water

175 g (6 oz) plain flour
25 g (1 oz) gluten flour

Dissolve the yeast in the water, add the flour and gluten, and form a dough. Knead this mixture for 2 minutes. This needs to rest overnight.

FOR THE BREAD DOUGH

300 ml (11 fl oz) water
2 teaspoons salt

175 g (6 oz) rye flour
275 g (10 oz) plain flour

Place all the ingredients along with the mother dough, in a mixing bowl and form the dough. Knead this for ten minutes. Allow the dough to prove for about 1 hour or until it has doubled in size. Knock the dough back down to its orginal size. If you have a kiln tile, you can make a round loaf to bake directly on the tile. The dough should be shaped up on a tray to prove and is then slid off the tray onto the hot tile to bake. Otherwise, line a loaf tin 20 x 10 cm (8 x 4 in) with greased greaseproof paper, place the dough in it and press it down hard into the corners. Allow either method another hour to prove until doubled in size in a warm, draught-free spot. Bake in an oven preheated to 200°C (400°F) for 1 hour or until bread sounds hollow when rapped on the base.

CHARCUTERIE

Charcuterie, the smoking and pickling of meats and the making of sausages, rillettes, pates and terrines, is a very considerable art. It is also an essential element of the Bayswater Brasserie kitchen and, possibly, the hardest for any home cook to master. Do not worry. Most brasseries, and Bayswater Brasserie is no exception, do not make all of their own charcuterie. In the French tradition they send out to experts, leaving their cooks to get on with their own culinary wonders. The Bayswater Brasserie does finish most of the chacuterie products it uses in its own drying cupboard.

One of the Bayswater's most popular breakfast dishes includes a spicy black pudding made by a local supplier. Australia's European population have demanded and established a fairly good range of charcuterie products.

Charcuterie was originally confined to the transformation of the noble pig into all kinds of delicacies. That is where the name comes from *chair cuit*, or cooked pork. Now it includes most other meats as well, including some game, ducks and geese. The good cook should have some charcuterie skills in their repertoire and we have included some of the simpler ones among the recipes in this book.

There are two excellent books which no kitchen library should be without. Jane Grigson's *Charcuterie and French Pork Cookery* and Linda Merinoff's *The Savoury Sausage—A Culinary Tour Around the World*.

SAUSAGES

Sausage making also takes a little time and patience, but there is nothing quite so delicious as your own home made sausage. Along with the pie, the Great Australian Sausage has always been one of life's mysteries. When you make your own there is no doubt at all about what company the ingredients have been keeping or where they have been.

To make your own snarlers you will need some special equipment. A good mincer is essential and so is a sausage funnel. A small sausage machine would be ideal, although some handy cooks manage to make an adequate sausage with nothing more than ingenuity and piping bags.

The home made sausage is greatly improved with fresh spices, bought in small quantities and ground just before use.

Skins and casings are obviously another essential and both artificial and natural varieties are available. The artificial skins are made out of edible collagen and sometimes inedible plastic which we suggest you give a miss. We only use the natural skins, which come mainly from sheep, pig's or beef entrails. The size of the casing depends on which part of the entrail is used. The casings for smaller sausages, for instance a chipolata, come from the small intestine of a sheep.

The casings, available from butcher's shops, are passed through rollers and flushed out with brine. They are stored either dry in salt or in a brine solution. Before using the skins they must be soaked in cold water for several hours. If not they will be brittle and may break while being filled.

PORK SAUSAGE

MAKES 12

700 g (1½ lb) lean pork meat, chopped
500 g (18 oz) pork back fat, chopped
3 teaspoons salt
2 teaspoons freshly ground black pepper

½ tsp nutmeg or mace
a length of soaked sausage skin about 3 m (10 ft) long

Mix the meat, fat and spices, making sure the meat is evenly distributed before passing it through the mincer fitted with a medium plate. For the large batches we make at the Brasserie ice is added to the mix to prevent the heat caused by mincing from cooking the meat. Thread the soaked skins onto the funnel, or the nozzle of the sausage machine. As you thread the skin on, about every 5 cm (2 in), prick or cut a tiny hole in the skin with a sharp knife, to prevent any air staying in the sausage as the meat is forced into the skin. The whole effect of this endeavour will be spoilt if you forget to finally tie a knot in the end of the skin.

Force all the meat into the skin, making sure it is neither too loosely nor too tightly packed. Tie off the filled skin, then pinch and twist into 12 individual sausage lengths.

DUCK SAUSAGE

MAKES 12

2 x 1.8 kg (4 lb) ducks, boned and skinned
200 ml (7 fl oz) mirin
500 g (18 oz) pork back fat
3 teaspoons salt
2 teaspoons freshly ground black pepper

1 teaspoon fennel seeds, toasted
1 pinch nutmeg or mace
1 length soaked sausage skin about 3 m (9 ft 10 in) long

Coarsely chop the duck meat and marinate for several hours in the mirin.

Combine with the other ingredients and follow the same method as for the pork sausage.

CHILLI BUTTER, SPINACH BUTTER AND MUSHROOM BUTTER

Flavoured butters are an incredibly versatile ingredient for supper dishes. They can be melted on lightly seared small birds, like squab, baby chickens or quail, or they can be grilled over oysters or other shellfish, served on the side of sauteed fish, dolloped onto a char-grilled steak, spread on toast, over scrambled or poached eggs, or combined into sauces.

If you are using these butters in a sauce, be careful to whisk them in at the end. If you boil the sauce with the butter in it the butter will separate.

All the butters make enough for 20 serves.

For this particular butter we use a very hot red chilli, so wear rubber gloves and treat it with enormous respect.

CHILLI BUTTER
175 g (6 oz) unsalted butter
a few drops olive oil
75 g (3 oz) small hot chillies, seeded

100 g (4 oz) Onion Puree (see page 128)
100 ml (3½ fl oz) red wine vinegar
½ bunch red basil leaves

Do not soften the butter over heat or there is a chance it will separate. Just let it stand at room temperature, then chop and mix it up with a wooden spatula until it is the right consistency.

Heat a few drops of olive oil and fry the chillies until they are soft. Add all the ingredients except the butter and basil leaves, and bring to the boil. Puree in a blender. Return to a clean pot, bring back to the boil and simmer, stirring constantly, until all the excess liquid has evaporated.

Leave the mixture until warm, then gradually incorporate the softened butter and basil leaves. Let this cool down to a rollable consistency, then roll in foil that has been sprinkled with a few drops of cold water. Refrigerate.

MUSHROOM BUTTER
This butter does not set as hard as the others. If you like it firmer, then add a greater quantity of the butter to the same amount of the other ingredients. Personally we prefer it creamy and rich in mushroom flavour as we have it here. The shiitake mushrooms could be replaced by dried cepes, mousserons or Italian porcilini.

50 g (2 oz) dried shiitake mushrooms
100 ml (3½ fl oz) sherry
150 ml (5 fl oz) Veal Stock (see page 22)
1 bunch tarragon leaves

1 tablespoon thick soy sauce
salt and pepper, to taste
175 g (6 oz) unsalted butter, softened

Cut the stems off the mushrooms and soak them in the sherry for at least 30 minutes. Heat the stock in a pot and cook the mushrooms and tarragon leaves in it for about 20 minutes or until most of the stock has reduced.

Puree the cooked mixture until completely smooth, adding the soy sauce, salt and pepper just before the end. Gradually incorporate the butter and roll as for Chilli Butter.

SPINACH BUTTER

Be careful not to overcook the spinach, the leaves should be steamed only until they are limp. Do not cook the sorrel at all or it will immediately turn the colour of an old brown paper bag.

1 clove garlic, peeled and chopped
1 tablespoon olive oil
2 bunches English spinach leaves

1 bunch sorrel leaves
salt and pepper, to taste
175 g (6 oz) unsalted butter, softened

Fry the garlic in hot olive oil until golden brown. Steam the spinach with a little water in a lidded pot until just limp. Drain the leaves and refresh them in cold water. Squeeze them out thoroughly. Puree the spinach, garlic, sorrel leaves and seasoning until completely smooth. Gradually incorporate the butter and roll as for Chilli Butter.

Using the Recipes

All the dishes in this book have been scaled down for the home kitchen. Obviously the Bayswater Brasserie works on a much larger scale, but all the dishes here have been tested in the smaller quantities.

We have set out the ingredients for each separate part of the dish followed by the method they require. To establish all the ingredients you need, read the whole recipe carefully to begin with.

Where ingredients have been given in weights or liquid measures it is because we feel the dish needs some precision as to their amount. Obviously your own intuition and taste will add its own style to our dishes. The way they are given here is how we like them, you may be able to make them better.

After all, if invention is a large part of all cooking it is the essence of the brasserie kitchen, and at the Bayswater Brasserie recipes are constantly being revised to improve them.

Breakfast

Those who love food must surely love breakfast first. Like all grand passions, though, the relationship is better prolonged if tempered with a little moderation. Not much in this chapter, for instance, is intended to begin every day of the week, since it is true in our hectic lifestyle that breakfast in the best sense of that meal is only an occasional delight. For the rest of the time we have to make do with a bowl of grain and a bite of toast with some juice and tea or coffee.

There are about as many breakfasts as there are cultures. In Europe, for instance, where the landscape might imperceptibly blend from one country into another, you will certainly know where you are when you face the first meal of the day.

The French sustain themselves with coffee and something baked—not always a croissant and probably more often a length of crunchy baguette split down the middle and buttered. The Belgians and Dutch could hardly contemplate a breakfast without cheese, while German traditionalists would not dream of facing the day without a generous helping of cold cuts or sausage. The Portuguese fancy tasty toppings for their toast. The English eat bacon and eggs, the Scots oatmeal, the Lancastrians grilled black puddings, the Welsh oat broth with buttermilk—or so tradition has it.

The Japanese have steamed rice or miso soup. The Thais eat a black rice pudding sweetened with coconut cream. The Chinese enjoy a kind of rice porridge with chunks of chicken or prawns, and in Sechuan province they pour hot chilli sauce over noodles. The Americans start their day with pancakes, crisp bacon and sweet syrup, or hash browns and eggs either once over lightly or sunny side up.

We can choose what we like from all of those. The traditional breakfast of our own Australian and New Zealand cultures was boiled mutton, or fried mutton chops with damper or a kind of fried dough cake. For the sake of national health, to say nothing of its palate, that is one tradition that is not missed.

For the weight and health conscious there are almost as many theories about breakfast as there are cultural variants of it. Some argue that in the morning the body's metabolism cannot sustain much food so breakfast should hardly exist. Others argue the complete reverse and one dogma goes "breakfast like a prince or princess, lunch like a King or Queen and dine like a poor person".

It is true that however splendid a breakfast might aspire to be, it is a meal that demands some sense and selectivity. Perhaps that is one of its greatest attractions. Since it is a meal that does not lend itself to great quantities or to a variety of courses, perfection, or its absence, is all the more obvious.

Bayswater Brasserie has always been a popular breakfast venue for late morning diners who enjoy a sumptuous and hearty start to the day. Its popularity is due to the fact that meals are cooked on the spot, not in advance, and the menu offers a wide selection of breakfast fare, including specially prepared charcuterie products, breads, croissants, muffins, compotes and jams.

The dishes in this chapter are all breakfast delights we enjoy. Some are demanding to prepare, some are simple, all of them are intended to be enjoyed on those few days when breakfast can be an event or those when it merges into something like an early lunch.

POACHED FRUIT AND RICOTTA

This dish takes some prior effort but it is well worthwhile, particularly if this is a breakfast that carries some caring messages for those who will enjoy it. Throwing caution and commonsense away, it could be served on a late summer morning with a glass of champagne or some chilly white and flinty wine or, for the more prudent, a tall cold glass of guava juice or buttermilk.

Ricotta cheese was traditionally made in southern Italy, in Campania and Apulia, from the whey left over from making provolone. Crumbly and rindless, it is often mixed with marsala and served as a dessert. It can be made with cow or goat's milk whey, and one delicious ricotta is made in New South Wales from ewe's milk.

SERVES 4–6

THE POACHING SYRUP

750 g (1¹/₃ lb) sugar

1 L (1 ²/₃ pts) water

juice and zest of 2 lemons

3–4 cinnamon sticks

1 vanilla pod, split

Mix all the ingredients together. Bring to the boil and cook until the sugar has dissolved. Strain it if you wish. Make the syrup in advance and store it in a cool place.

THE FRUIT AND RICOTTA

3 medium freestone peaches

2–3 nectarines

4–6 blood plums

3 pears, peeled and cored

1 quince, peeled and seeded

1 punnet of raspberries

500 g (18 oz) ricotta

Note: Most fruit is suitable for poaching—figs, tamarillos, guavas are excellent. Passionfruit is an equally useful substitute for the berries, or as an accompaniment.

Prepare, to your taste, just ripe freestone peaches, nectarines, plums and pears. Bring the syrup to the boil and cook the fruits, adding the firmest and largest fruit first. When the fruit is cooked, add the raspberries or whatever small berries take your fancy. These do not need to be cooked; they are included for colour and flavour. Chill the cooked fruits in the syrup.

Serve the fruit in bowls, topped with a generous scoop of ricotta. Reserve a little of the syrup to ladle over the cheese just before serving.

FRANCES'S TOASTED GRAINS AND NUTS

In North America this breakfast mix enjoys the cosy name, "crunchy granola". This can be an everyday breakfast. It is much more easily digested than muesli and, to our taste, ten times more enjoyable. It keeps well in an airtight container, so make whatever quantity you can store. The oil version stores better than the butter.

MAKES ENOUGH FOR 15 GOOD SERVES—2.5 kg (5½ lb)

200 g (7 oz) apricots
200 g (7 oz) raisins
200 g (7 oz) dates, pitted
200 g (7 oz) currants
200 g (7 oz) butter or 200 ml (7 fl oz) vegetable oil
500 ml (18 fl oz) honey

150 g (5 oz) unsalted blanched almonds
150 g (5 oz) unsalted cashews
150 g (5 oz) unsalted pistachios, shelled
500 g (18 oz) rolled oats
150 g (5 oz) bran flakes
150 g (5 oz) wheat germ
3 tablespoons dessicated coconut

You can add in whatever dried fruits you fancy but select these with care. If they are not well done and are too hard, they can completely destroy the texture of the whole mix. Chop the larger fruits well.

Heat the butter or oil together with the honey until the honey has completely melted. Mix the grains and nuts together in a large bowl, then toss the honey and butter or oil mix through until they are thoroughly dressed. Spread the mixture evenly over a high-sided baking tray and toast slowly until golden brown in an oven heated to around 150°C (300°F). Let it cool and mix in the chopped fruits. Store in an airtight container.

The toasted grains are served moistened with milk, buttermilk, yoghurt, soy milk or fruit juice and can be served with poached or fresh fruits.

BRIOCHE

There can be endless arguments about the relative merits of brioche or croissant as a breakfast bread—outside France that is, where brioches in their various wonderful forms would never be served as part of the breakfast menu.

For the home baker, the argument is easily solved. The complex process of the croissant dough takes forever and only the fortunate and obsessive few with an entire kitchen day at their disposal can make the time available to manufacture it. The light and buttery brioche is both relatively easy to make and equally delicious.

MAKES 1 x 1 kg (2 lb 3 oz) LOAF OR 12 BUNS

15 g (½ oz) fresh yeast

250 ml (9 fl oz) tepid milk

500 g (18 oz) plain flour

1 teaspoon sugar

1 teaspoon salt

6 egg yolks

165 g (5½ oz) butter, soft, not melting

2 egg yolks, beaten, for glazing

Dissolve the yeast in the tepid milk. Put the flour, sugar and salt into a bowl, make a well in the centre and mix in the 6 egg yolks and yeast mixture. Mix the softened butter quickly through the dough and knead until it is shiny.

Roll the dough into a loaf shape and press it into a 30 x 12.5 cm (12 x 5 in) tin or divide it up into the more traditional small buns—about 75 g (3 oz) to a portion. The Parisian brioche is made with a small ball of dough on top of a larger ball.

Let the dough rise until nearly doubled in size. Glaze the loaf or buns with the 2 egg yolks and in an oven preheated to 200°C (390°F) bake the buns for 20 minutes or the loaf for 1 hour.

MUFFINS AND LEMON CURD

The muffin appears in two quite different guises. In England it is a kind of flat, round yeast dough roll, toasted and buttered and usually enjoyed at tea time. The Americans cook theirs in deep tins and instead of yeast to raise the mix, they use baking powder.

These muffins are the American sort and an excellent breakfast companion they make too. Be warned though, the only muffin worth eating is a fresh muffin, so do not bake more than you intend to eat immediately.

MAKES 12 MUFFINS

1 tablespoon each of flour and butter, for
   greasing the muffin tins

125 g (4 oz) butter

125 g (4 oz) sugar

2 eggs

300 g (11 oz) plain flour

2½ teaspoons baking powder

a pinch of salt

125 ml (4 fl oz) milk

Grease and flour the muffin tins.

Cream the butter and sugar together and add the eggs one at a time. Sieve the flour, baking powder and salt and add it in a stream from a funnel of greaseproof paper. Mix in the milk.

At this point, add whatever fruit you choose. For the whole mix you will need these proportions.

BANANA AND DATE

1 banana, chopped

125 g (4 oz) dates, pitted, chopped and
   combined with the banana

BLUEBERRIES

1 punnet of blueberries

If you like, divide the muffin mixture and make a variety of fruit muffins in the one batch.

Bake the muffins in an oven preheated to 180°C (350°F) for about 20 minutes.

THE LEMON CURD

4 lemons

6 eggs

125 g (4 oz) butter, chopped

150 g (5 oz) sugar

Grate the zest from the lemons and squeeze the juice. Mix all the curd ingredients together and heat slowly to boiling point in a double boiler. Take off the heat immediately the first bubble appears and pass it through a sieve.

ORANGE AND YOGHURT PANCAKES

Pancakes, the French prefer to call them crepes, are almost as versatile a dish as omelettes. They can be sweet or savoury. They are fine at breakfast, supper or in between. Some of the nicest are to be bought at footpath stalls in almost any French city.

Also, like the omelette, they are a good test of basic stove top skills. Toss them if you will, but the prudent cook will flip them with a large flat spatula. They also need an excellent pan or a flat griddle.

In this recipe, yoghurt is used in the batter in place of the more traditional milk or beer.

SERVES 4–6

225 g (8 oz) plain flour

50 g (2 oz) sugar

1 teaspoon baking powder

2 eggs

juice of 2 oranges

150 ml (5 fl oz) yoghurt

75 g (3 oz) butter, melted

2 tablespoons clarified butter

Sieve the flour into a bowl, then add the sugar and baking powder. Make a well in the centre, then add the eggs and orange juice, mixing these to a smooth creamy consistency. Stir in the yoghurt and then the melted butter. Let the batter rest for at least 30 minutes. (Traditional recipes suggest up to 2 hours.)

Cook the pancakes in a hot pan with an absolute minimum of clarified butter. Cook the first side until the top looks as if it is steamed through, then toss or flip and cook the other side. Make sure your pancakes don't look as though they've had a month at Bondi—a pale golden brown will do. Serve with pouring cream or yoghurt and liberal amounts of mixed berries.

PORRIDGE WITH BLACK SUGAR AND GINGER POWDER

The Celts gave porridge to the world. They thought it a wonderfully sustaining dish, although their view of its merits is not one shared by gourmets of other races. In his *Dictionary of the English Language*, for example, the acerbic Dr Johnson described the oats from which the dish is made as "a grain which in England is generally given to horses, but in Scotland supports the people".

Despite the bad press writers like Johnson and Charles Dickens gave it— it was a second serving of a variety of porridge that poor Oliver Twist begged for in the workhouse—porridge makes a marvellous breakfast. The delicious smell that greets the diner when the lid is lifted on this dish might even have changed the difficult doctor's opinion.

SERVES 4–6

200 g (7 oz) rolled oats

milk, for soaking oats

a pinch of salt

1 L (1²/₃ pts) milk

3 tablespoons butter

½ teaspoon powdered ginger

4 tablespoons black sugar, or to taste

Soak the oats in milk overnight, then drain and add a pinch of salt.

Bring the milk to the boil and add the rolled oats. Return to the boil and simmer for 15 minutes. Serve the porridge in lidded bowls. Top each with a knob of butter and a good pinch of powdered ginger, and sprinkle with black sugar. Pour milk or cream around the edge and serve with the lid on.

Note: Black sugar, which is actually a very dark brown, is the most natural and least refined of sugars, keeping most of its molasses. Home made coconut size and shaped lumps of this basic sugar used to be sold as a kind of fudge-like sweet in the markets in Fiji and maybe still are. In Australia, Indian shops are the most likely suppliers of the best and darkest black sugar

GOAT CHEESE TART

With a curious perversity North Americans call a tart an open or single crusted pie, which of course a pie can never be since the essential element of a pie is its lid, so when the pie is open it becomes, a tart! The English and French sometimes further confuse the dish by calling it a flan.

The tart goes back at least to the Middle Ages, from which time a great many recipes survived. Playing cards belong to the same period which is no doubt the reason why it was tarts that the Queen of Hearts made and Jack pinched.

English tarts are most often sweet but in France some of the oldest tart recipes include cheese, sometimes in combination with fruit. In northern and eastern France and in Corsica cheese tarts remain a traditional dish.

Goat's cheese tart is an ideal dish for brunch or elegant picnic lunch.

SERVES 8

300 g (11 oz) puff pastry
a little butter for greasing the tin
6 eggs
500 ml (18 fl oz) cream

salt and pepper
2 x 150 g (5 oz) Fromage Fermier goat's cheese
1 bunch chervil, chopped
½ bunch chives, chopped

To make the base, roll out the pastry to 3 mm (⅛ in) thickness, then line a 25 cm (10 in) greased tart mould. Prick the pastry and carefully line it with foil filled with rice. Let this rest for about 45 minutes and then bake in an oven preheated to 180°C (350°F) for about 25 minutes or until the pastry sets. Remove the foil and rice and cook further until the pastry is cooked right through.

While the base is baking, break the eggs into a bowl and whisk with the cream, seasoning to your taste. Grate the cheese and sprinkle over the cooked base, adding the herbs on top. Pour in the egg and cream mix. Cover with a sheet of baking paper and cook at 150°C (300°F) for 35 minutes.

HASH BROWN POTATOES

There are a number of different ways to make this dish and the majority of them have given it a bad name—more like mush grey than hash brown. This is probably the most authentic method and it's the one that works for us. Use 2 medium potatoes per person.

SERVES 6

12 medium potatoes, peeled
200 g (7 oz) clarified butter

salt and pepper, to taste

Choose waxy rather than floury potatoes, sequoias or pontiacs for example. Boil the potatoes in plenty of salted water and set aside to cool.

Heat a heavy-based pan or solid grill plate and add the clarified butter. While this is heating, coarsely grate the potatoes and dry them off slightly, but don't let them stand for too long or they will oxidise to an unpleasant brown colour.

Press the potatoes into the pan and season them with salt and freshly crushed coarse black pepper. Cook them steadily, being careful not to blacken the edges and making sure a crust is forming. There should be enough juice from the potatoes to ensure crusting. Set the pan aside and cover with a lid to steam the potatoes. After 5 minutes turn them out, reheat the pan, add some more clarified butter and cook them on the other side until brown. Serve these with eggs, sausages, sauteed liver or mushrooms.

A PLAIN OMELETTE

There could hardly be a dish more wonderful in its simplicity than an omelette. Nor is there one that makes more demands on a cook's skills. Hands, eyes and nose are all engaged in the construction of the perfect omelette and, it should really go without saying, there is no other kind of omelette worth serving.

The omelette is one of the oldest recorded dishes still to make its way to the ordinary table. Oddly enough, for all its simplicity, it is also a dish that carries a considerable amount of romantic mythology and which figures in a number of stories about kings, emperors and courtesans.

One of the oldest surviving recipes is that of the Roman gourmet, Apicius, who certainly did not just stumble on the dish, since his account of it contains two things many an omelette fancier today will still insist on—the finished product being turned out of the pan still slightly runny, and the addition of a small amount of liquid to the mix, in Apicius's case milk.

The best omelettes begin with the best pans. The ideal shape has rounded sloping shoulders to let the eggs spread when tilted during cooking and to allow the finished, folded omelette to easily turn out onto the plate. The omelette pan must be exactly the right size for the number of eggs (an omelette fancier might have two or three) and must never be washed with water or used for anything else. For the omelette in this recipe a pan about 18 cm (7 in) in diameter would be about right.

The surface must be perfect. There are all kinds of patent non-stick omelette pans about and no doubt their owners and inventors love them dearly. The pan preferred here is a heavy-based black steel pan cured by the cook.

To cure, fill the pan with salt, then burn it steadily over medium heat for at least an hour or so, until the surface has become smooth and of an even, bluish colour. Throw the salt out into a bowl and let it cool before dumping it, otherwise you run the risk of setting your bin on fire. Let the pan cool a little and rub with a small quantity of vegetable oil. Do not leave any of this in the pan but do make sure the surface has and keeps a slight sheen. From now on never let any water touch its surface. To keep it clean, wipe it out after cooking with a dry kitchen towel while still hot and if there is any residue to remove, scour it off with coarse salt.

TO MAKE A BASIC OMELETTE FOR ONE YOU WILL NEED

3 fresh eggs   salt and pepper

a knob of butter

Fold the eggs together with a fork or small whisk. Do not beat them. Whisk in the water and seasoning. Drop the butter in the heated pan and while it is still foaming but not yet coloured, pour in the eggs and immediately stir them with a fork while tilting the pan and moving it around. Keep lifting the eggs around the edge and drawing the fork through the centre of the mix so the runny mixture can keep folding under and across the heat. If your pan is right the plate of cooking egg should move freely on the surface without sticking anywhere.

When you judge the mixture cooked—by eye and nose—it should still have a runny yellow surface and a nutty eggy smell—fold it in half and tip it onto a well warmed plate. Some cuisines serve their omelettes flat and maybe they are right to do so since the name seems to derive from the Latin for 'flat plate'.

Excessive good manners can ruin an omelette, since the cooking process does not really end until it begins to cool, so arrange for each one to be eaten as soon as it hits the plate.

Within reason you can put anything you like inside your omelette. One famous omelette book gives 314 different versions of the dish. Just keep in mind that the best fillings are those which need little cooking, or which are pre-cooked just enough to need only reheating inside the omelette in its final stages.

BRANDADE

B randade, a delicious puree of salt cod, is a traditional dish of Provence and Languedoc. It makes a splendid companion to a basic omelette or it can be served in its own right with croutons or a poached egg.

SERVES 8–10

600 g (18 oz) salt cod (roughly one small side)
200 ml (7 fl oz) tepid milk
100 ml (3½ fl oz) virgin olive oil

1 large pinch ground white pepper
2 small potatoes, peeled, boiled and pureed
sea salt, to taste

Soak the salt cod overnight, changing the water a couple of times. Drain and cover the fish with fresh water, then poach gently for 10 minutes. Remove the bones and skin. Puree the cod in a blender, adding the milk and oil in alternate streams. Season with the pepper and mix through the potato. Add salt only if necessary.

To serve a flat omelette, arrange the cod puree around the omelette on a plate and sprinkle liberally with Italian parsley. Or serve it simply topped with parsley and fried croutons, or garnished with a light dusting of grated hard cheese, browning under the grill or salamander just before serving.

POACHED EGGS ON SALAD LEAVES WITH
SMOKED OCEAN TROUT

F or a late breakfast or early lunch on a sunny summer's day there could hardly be any more appropriate dish than this elegant combination of poached eggs, fresh leaves and sweet smoked ocean trout. For a variation try any other garnish that takes your fancy. A simple mousse of trout, for instance, spread on a dry, crisp crouton and tucked into the leaves. Or spinach leaves, nuts and crisply fried bacon. Sprinkle salmon roe through the leaves, or Beluga caviar if you feel outrageously affluent or if there is perhaps some emotional transaction hanging on this meal.

SERVES 6

POACHED EGGS

12 eggs
sea salt and freshly ground pepper

The freshest eggs poach best since these have the largest proportion of thick white and will spread the least. As eggs age the amount of thick white decreases, the egg becomes runnier and the yolk more prone to breaking. A simple test for egg freshness is to watch how fast the egg sinks in a bowl of water. The faster the fresher, and a bad egg will float.

Break the egg into a cup just before you slide it into the water. Exposing the white to air for any length of time will have the same effect on it as ageing. The water in the saucepan should be at a rolling boil as the eggs go in, to quickly coagulate the outside and restrain the yolk. A turbulent boil will strip the thin parts of the white away into spidery skeins.

A small amount of vinegar or lemon juice—about one part to seven of water— will help speed coagulation and retain the egg's shape, but it will also add its own note to the flavour. The eggs will reduce the heat, so bring the water back up to the rolling boil and then let it drop off to a simmer. Cook for 2–3 minutes or use your eye to judge when the white of the egg has set without overcooking the yolk to a pale, sulphurous yellow pellet.

THE SALAD
1 head of cos lettuce
1 shoot of witloof
½ bunch watercress leaves
6 small pieces from the white leaves of curly endive

2 handfuls mache leaves
¼ bundle of Hijiki seaweed (soak in cold water until softened, dress separately with a little rice vinegar and toasted sesame seeds to taste)

Wash all the leaves in chilly water and carefully dry them. If preparing the leaves in advance, store them somewhere cool. Never add dressing until immediately before serving.

THE DRESSING
juice and zest of 1 lemon
salt and pepper, to taste

1 tablespoon rice vinegar
2 tablespoons grape seed oil
2 tablespoons olive oil

Mix together the lemon juice and zest, salt and pepper, and vinegar. Gradually whisk the oils into the mixture. Check the seasoning. This quantity will be more than enough for the leaves. It is always better to underdress the leaves than swamp them. If anything ever called for an elegant understatement it is a salad dressing.

THE OCEAN TROUT
450 g (16 oz) smoked ocean trout

This will give you four or five good slices per serve.

To serve, dress the salad leaves, arrange the seaweed and slices of ocean trout over the leaves. Place 2 poached eggs in the middle of each salad. Season with sea salt and freshly ground pepper at the last minute.

SOFT-BOILED EGG ON AN OKRA AND STRACCHINO SALAD

Okra is an African vegetable which African slaves took to America and from there, quite recently, the rest of us have taken it up. Traditionally it is the basic ingredient of stews. In this recipe its distinctive flavour can be enjoyed for itself.

Originally from Lombardy, stracchino is a soft centred, washed rind cheese made from cow's milk and is usually quite high in fat.

SERVES 4–6

250 ml (9 fl oz) grape seed oil	*2 bunches rocket leaves, washed*
500 g (18 oz) small okras, split	*250 g (9 oz) mature stracchino, sliced*
4 tablespoons polenta	*salt and pepper, to taste*
2 fresh eggs per serve	*4 tablespoons olive oil*
1 bunch watercress leaves, washed	*2 tablespoons balsamic vinegar*

Heat the oil in a deep pan. Toss the okra in the polenta and fry for about 3 minutes or until dark brown.

While the okra is cooking, start the eggs in a pot of cold water and bring steadily to the boil. Keep them in a rolling boil for 5 minutes, then turn them carefully out into cold water for 1 minute more to stop them cooking.

Let the okra cool a little, then toss with the salad leaves and stracchino. Season with the salt and pepper, and sprinkle the olive oil and vinegar over. Carefully peel the eggs and serve on top of the warm salad. If you like, just before serving, split each egg.

CORN FRITTERS WITH RED CAPSICUMS AND CRISPY BACON

This makes a superb weekend breakfast. In Australia and New Zealand the fritters are traditionally made with creamed corn from a can. A much better version is made from fresh corn cooked through on the cob, trimmed and made into a cream.

Serve the fritters with crispy bacon. The Dutch have a marvellous thin bacon, which seems to have no other name than "breakfast bacon", for this purpose. Perhaps a version of it can be hunted down for this dish. Choose your bacon with care and insist on it being lean and thin. Vacuum-packed bacon is hardly ever successfully fried until crisp so avoid it.

SERVES 4–6

THE CORN FRITTERS

3 corn cobs, kernels removed

75 ml (3 fl oz) milk

75 g (3 oz) butter

75 g (3 oz) plain flour

2 eggs

2 red capsicums, grilled, peeled and sliced

a few drops of tabasco

salt and freshly ground black pepper

200 g (7 oz) clarified butter

Cook the corn kernels in salted water to cover for about 1 hour or until quite soft. Puree half the corn in a food processor and mix this together with the whole kernels.

Heat the milk and butter together. Pour in the flour from a funnel made with kitchen paper. Stirring constantly, cook the mixture for 3–4 minutes or until it comes away from the sides of the pan. Mix the corn through the mixture, then add the eggs one at a time, thoroughly mixing after each. Mix through the sliced capsicums and tabasco, then season with plenty of ground black pepper and salt.

THE BACON

400 g (14 oz) bacon, thinly sliced

Dry each rasher of bacon carefully, then just moisten slightly with plain water. Lay the bacon on a cake rack, which is sitting in a tray to catch any fat. Cook for 10 minutes or until crisp in an oven preheated to 200°C (400°F). Keep warm in the oven on kitchen paper.

To serve the fritters heat the clarified butter in a large steel pan. Oil 2 dessertspoons and drop spoonfuls of the mixture into the hot clarified butter. Turn each fritter over when it becomes golden brown. These may have to be cooked in 2–3 batches.

Drain well and serve with the crispy bacon, slices of raw tomato, and tabasco on the side.

CORNED BEEF HASH WITH A POACHED EGG

This dish will also do for an early lunch.

It is not always easy to find a good corned beef so you may like to pickle your own. Good corned beef is essential even though this dish is basically a mixture of leftovers. Commercially corned beef is usually a cut from the silverside, but brisket or rump make excellent substitutes.

SERVES 6

THE BRINE

125 g (4 oz) rock salt
125 g (4 oz) brown sugar
1 teaspoon saltpetre
1 L (1⅔ pts) water

125 ml (4 fl oz) molasses
1 teaspoon whole spice
1 teaspoon pepper
1 teaspoon mace
6 cloves garlic, mashed

Dissolve the salt, sugar and saltpetre in 250 ml (9 fl oz) of water and add to the remaining ingredients with the rest of the water.

THE MEAT AND COURT BOUILLON

1 kg (2 lb 3 oz) rump or brisket of beef
1½ L (2½ pts) water
2 medium onions, quartered
2 cloves

½ teaspoon black peppercorns
3 medium carrots, peeled and chopped
juice of 2 lemons
2 bay leaves
a sprig of fresh thyme

Pierce the meat, then immerse it in the brine and let it stand in a cool place for 10–12 days.

To cook the finished cut, cover it with cold water and bring it to the boil. Simmer for 10 minutes, then discard the water.

Put the onions studded with the cloves, black peppercorns, carrots, juice, bay leaves and thyme into the 1½ L (2½ pts) water. Boil for 10 minutes, then pour over the meat. Depending on the size of the cut, simmer it gently for another 4 hours.

Slices of corned beef, warm or cold, are delicious served with a salad or in a picnic sandwich, but we are on about hash here, so to begin that, chop the beef to serve six hungry breakfasters.

THE HASH

1 kg (2 lb 3 oz) corned beef, finely chopped
100 g (4 oz) butter
2 small onions, finely chopped
2 large potatoes, boiled and chopped

1 small butternut pumpkin or left over sweet potatoes, or both, cooked and chopped
salt and pepper, to taste
¼ bunch Italian parsley, chopped

Mix together all the hash ingredients except the parsley. Heat a heavy-based pan and add a generous knob of butter. When it stops foaming and before it begins to colour, press the hash down into the pan. Let a crust slowly build, turning the hash over like a pancake to preserve the crust. To help the crust form, after the mix is pressed into the hot pan you can add a little boiling water or consomme around the edges.

Cut it into wedges and serve with toast, on top of tomatoes sliced into a bowl and topped with a perfectly poached egg. Liberally sprinkle the whole with the parsley.

BLACK PUDDING WITH SAUTEED APPLES AND FRIED MASHED POTATO

There could hardly be a more substantial winter breakfast than this. Sadly, many people miss out on this dish through an aversion to the idea of eating what is more plainly called, blood sausage. While their distaste for the idea is understandable, those who can courageously engage their palate with the dish itself will have no trouble eating it again.

It is a sausage that has a truly amazing number of varieties. The French, for example, are said by Larousse to have about as many versions of this as there are pork butchers. In Amsterdam, the little Surinam cafes around the Albert Cuyp market have a wonderfully spicy black pudding which seems to promote a demand for that other wonderful Dutch product, beer, but perhaps not for breakfast.

SERVES 4–6

6 small cooking apples
75 g (3 oz) butter
150 ml (5 fl oz) apple cider
salt and pepper, to taste

4 large Pontiac potatoes, cooked and mashed
75 g (3 oz) clarified butter
3 x 150 g (5 oz) black puddings

Peel and seed the apples and cut them into eighths. Melt the butter in a heavy-based saucepan until it stops foaming, then brown the apples on both sides. Reduce the heat, splash in the cider, cover the pan and steam the apples over a low heat until firm, but cooked.

Season the mashed potatoes and fry them in the clarified butter, turning them well until they are golden brown all over. Slice the black puddings into 1 cm (¼ in) slices and warm through under a hot grill.

To serve, arrange the apples, black pudding and potato on the plate and glaze with the apple juices. It might be necessary to add a little more cider to thin the juices.

SCRAPPLE AND HERBED SCRAMBLED EGGS

Sometimes called Pan Haus, this dish from the southern USA most likely had its origins in Europe. The notion, though, of making a meat and grain mash to fry is not a particularly common one in modern European cuisine.

The pork bits for this dish can come from any part of the beast—head, liver, trotters or belly for instance. A good proportion of gelatinous pieces like trotter or cheek can add considerable character to the finished scrapple.

Serve the scrapple with herbed scrambled eggs and toast.

SERVES 4–6

THE SCRAPPLE

1 veal tongue
1 pork trotter
150 g (5 oz) pork liver
400 g (14 oz) pork meat

2 L (3½ pts) Chicken Stock (see page 23)
salt and pepper, to taste
75 g (3 oz) corn meal
75 g (3 oz) oatmeal
50 ml (2 fl oz) oil, or 60 g (2 oz) bacon fat

Cover the meat with stock. Bring this to the boil and skim. Simmer for 3–4 hours, topping up the liquid as it reduces. Strain the meat, let it cool, then chop or mince it through a coarse blade.

Weigh or measure equal parts of the meat and the cooking liquid. You should have about 400 g (14 oz) of meat and 400 mls (14 fl oz) of liquid. Bring the mixture to the boil, seasoning with the salt and pepper. Add the corn meal and oatmeal as if you were cooking polenta, pouring in a stream from a funnel of kitchen paper.

Bring this mixture back to the boil, stirring, and being careful not to get splattered by the bubbling mixture which will behave like a Rotorua mudpool. Pour the mixture into a flat tray, cover and let cool. Cut the cooled scrapple into long strips and fry in oil or bacon fat until browned on both sides.

THE HERBED SCRAMBLED EGGS

8–12 eggs, or 2 eggs per serve
150 ml (5 fl oz) cream
50 g (2 oz) butter
salt and pepper, to taste

1 tablespoon chopped chives
1 tablespoon chopped chervil
1 tablespoon chopped parsley
1 tablespoon chopped basil
4–6 slices of bread for toast

Break up the eggs together without beating too much air into them. Heat the cream in a small stainless steel pan with the butter. Season the eggs with salt and pepper and mix the herbs through them. Add the eggs to the cream and butter, stirring constantly. Do not overcook. They should stand up on the toast, yet still be quite wet.

Lunch

The nicest interpretation that can be put on the American expression "out to lunch" is that if lunch is your thing, you must have plenty of disposable time on your hands. Perhaps that is why Manhattan is known as the one city on earth that serves lunch twenty-four hours of the day.

There is something leisurely about lunch. Not the lunch seized from a deli in a brown paper bag and consumed on the move, but the classic lunch savoured in repose. Perhaps the finest distillation of that notion is the Impressionist painter Claude Monet's image, *Dejeuner sur l'Herbe*—two elegant gentlemen and two beautiful women enjoy a simple repast in a sylvan paradise. We might actually call that particular lunch a picnic and its attraction is no doubt enhanced by the dress, or lack of it, of two of the diners.

Monet is not saying something about lunch, but about a classic lifestyle recalled in what was for him a modern setting. It is no accident though that he chose lunch as the occasion, since perhaps no other meal is so much about a style of life—in our times, for the most part, straightforward and free from ritual and formality.

Like a great many things about food the word lunch, used to refer to a meal at the middle of the day, has evolved from something entirely different. The word originally meant a thick lump or hunk of something, so on the way to its modern usage, it may have first come to mean a slab of bread or meat consumed to ward off hunger between breakfast and dinner—dinner, of course, being the main meal eaten by the majority of English people at midday.

In France the word lunch was introduced a century or so ago to refer to a particular version of *dejeuner*—their proper midday meal. It was what we might call a buffet, or that line of boring and sloppy dishes that passes for a smorgasbord— a selection of food to be consumed standing up. It appeared as luncheon in reference to an informal midday meal in England in the eighteenth century, and by the middle of the last century became shortened to lunch.

The lunch style, if such a thing can be isolated from general brasserie cuisine, is one that most typifies the Bayswater Brasserie. It is also our most popular with regulars who like to pop in for a quick one-course meal. For this reason our menu provides a wide selection of courses, many of which are entire meals in themselves, so diners can construct a menu to suit their appetite. Because of the flexibility this allows, we have offered a larger number of recipes in this chapter than in the others. Of course, many of the dishes here will do as well for dinners and picnics as they do for lunch.

FISH SOUP ROUILLE

The rouille in this dish is a delicious garlic and red capsicum mayonnaise. Traditionally rouille is served with Bouillabaise or the Provençale fish soup Bourride. Elizabeth David mentions a saffron eel stew with rouille and croutons.

If you have a taste for a hotter version than this, substitue some hot chilli peppers for some of the sweet red one. For this dish we have added a few saffron threads and a little lemon juice.

The soup is made from various white fish of different sizes. After cooking, the fish and the vegetables are all pushed through a mouli or sieve—this will thicken the soup slightly.

SERVES 8–10

THE SOUP

150 mls (5 fl oz) olive oil

300 g (11 oz) whiting

200 g (7 oz) red spot whiting or silver dollar
   fish

200 g (7 oz) red mullet

250 g (9 oz) snapper

400 g (14 oz) flathead

3 medium onions, sliced

2 medium leeks, sliced

stalks from ½ bunch parsley

5 medium tomatoes, chopped

2 bay leaves, fresh or dried

salt and pepper, to taste

200 ml (7 fl oz) white wine

juice of 1 lemon

1 L (1²/₃ pts) water

basil leaves

1 loaf country bread, for croutons

Heat the olive oil in a large pan and saute the fish and onions without letting them colour. Add the leeks, parsley, tomatoes, bay leaves and seasoning, then cover with the wine, lemon juice and water.

Simmer the soup for 30 minutes, skimming it from time to time. Add the basil leaves in the last 5 minutes, then check and correct the seasoning. Take the soup off the flame and let it cool slightly. Pass all of it through a food mill or sieve with a medium-fine net into a clean pan. Bring it back to the boil, then maintain just below a simmer.

While the soup is cooking, make the croutons and the rouille. The best croutons are made from thinnish slices of rough country bread. Use quite large slices and dry them in the oven at about 140°C (275°F) for 15–20 minutes or until dry.

THE ROUILLE

2 cloves garlic, peeled

salt and pepper, to taste

1 large red capsicum, grilled and peeled

1 small chilli, seeds and stalk removed

4 threads of saffron

2 egg yolks

juice of ½ a lemon

250 mls (9 fl oz) olive oil

The rouille can be made in a mortar but it is much simpler in a food processor. Make a paste with the garlic, salt, pepper, red capsicum, chilli and saffron. Add the egg yolks and lemon juice. Slowly blend this mixture, dribbling in the oil drop by drop until it has all been added.

To serve, place a crouton in each bowl and spoon a generous dollop of the rouille on top, then pour the soup over it.

Note: As the recipe for rouille makes a larger quantity than required, store any remaining rouille in the refrigerator.

BLUE SWIMMER CRAB BISQUE

The traditional bisque is made with lobster and shellfish. According to Larousse it was a Spanish soup originally made with boiled meat and game and, sometime later, with small game birds. This version is quite a thick soup with an appealing silky finish. For a winter lunch it can be finished with cream which enhances the texture. On a hot day, or if you are worried about calories, leave the cream out and thicken it with either rice or potatoes.

Finishing the dish requires a fair bit of hard work as the crab shells have to be ground up with all the other ingredients and then rubbed through a sieve. Without this final step the soup has none of its distinctive character.

SERVES 8–10

THE SOUP

4 blue swimmer crabs

1.5 L (2½ pts) Fish Stock (see page 23)

100 ml (3½ fl oz) olive oil

3 onions, roughly chopped

1 leek, roughly chopped

1 clove garlic, roughly chopped

4 tomatoes, roughly chopped

50 g (2 oz)rice

2 bay leaves

½ bunch parsley stalks

75 ml (3 fl oz) brandy or port

150 ml (5 fl oz) cream

croutons, to serve

Smash and chop the crabs, leaving the claws intact, then poach the claws in the stock and set them aside. Saute the smashed crabs in the olive oil for 8 minutes, then add the onions, leek, garlic and tomatoes, and saute for 2 minutes more.

Stir in the rice, bay leaves and parsley stalks, cover with the stock and simmer for 2 hours.

Let the cooked soup cool slightly and then either grind the ingredients by hand or blend in a powerful blender. With a wooden mushroom, push the soup through a sieve into a clean saucepan. Pour any remaining liquid through the sieve, then add the brandy or port. Bring the bisque back to the boil. Simmer for 10 minutes, then add the cream. Do not let it reboil.

Serve the soup in a large bowl with the croutons and the reserved claws, which have been reheated in some of the fish stock.

PEA AND SAUSAGE SOUP

This is a traditional Dutch dish and the brown cafes in Amsterdam serve wonderful versions of it. You can chop all kinds of smoked sausage and other charcuterie meats into it. Here we suggest kransky, although any other smoked sausages will do, pork kassler, salted pork, and pig's trotters. It is the kind of soup that can go on being added to as long as the basic stock lasts.

It's a midwinter dish and just the thing to make for skiing or to take on a winter picnic. Serve it with squares of bread fried in butter or large chunks of rye or black bread. It is definitely not the sort of soup that needs half-hearted treatment, so offer it with liberal amounts of freshly ground black pepper on top.

SERVES 8–10

250 g (9 oz) kassler	2 medium potatoes, roughly chopped
150 g (5 oz) kransky	2 medium onions, roughly chopped
2 pig's trotters	1 large leek, roughly chopped
250 g (9 oz) salt pork	1 bulb of celeriac, peeled and chopped
400 g (14 oz) bacon or ham bones	800 g (1¾ lb) fresh peas, shelled
1 L (1²/₃ pts) Chicken Stock (see page 23)	50 g (2 oz) unsalted butter
2 bay leaves	salt and pepper, to taste

Put all the meat in cold water and bring it to the boil, then immediately discard the water and cover the meat with the chicken stock. Add the bay leaves and cook for 3 hours. Strain and set the meat aside, reserving the stock.

Sweat all the vegetables, except the peas, in butter until the onions become clear, then add the reserved stock. Simmer until the potatoes are soft. Add the peas and simmer for 10 minutes making sure they do not lose their colour. Check the seasoning and adjust if necessary.

Meanwhile chop the meats, slice the sausage, and discard any bones. Remove the bay leaves and puree the cooked vegetables with all the stock in a blender. Put the puree into a clean pan with the chopped meats and sliced sausage, and bring back to the boil. If the soup is too thick, use a little extra stock or water to thin it.

OXTAIL AND TOMATO SOUP WITH STOUT

Chunks of gelatinous oxtail served in a clear black soup is definitely a robust winter lunch. The original dish is traditionally English, so adding a bottle of cream stout to finish it off keeps the whole thing very much in the same culture. The Italians also enjoy oxtail, although they are likely to eat it as a stew braised with brisket and pork belly.

The finished dish should be generously thick with oxtail, and served over a couple of tablespoons of chopped tomato with some extra virgin olive oil added to it. Top it with a liberal handful of chopped Italian parsley.

SERVES 8–10

1.2 kg (2¾ lb) oxtails
100 g (4 oz) flour, seasoned with salt and pepper
100 ml (3½ fl oz) vegetable oil
3 medium onions
2 medium carrots
2 sticks celery
2 medium leeks
1 large turnip

1.5 L (2½ pts) Veal Stock (see page 22), brought to the boil
5 medium tomatoes
3 fresh bay leaves
salt and pepper, to taste
1 x 350 ml (12 fl oz) bottle cream stout
3 medium tomatoes, peeled, seeded and chopped
½ bunch Italian parsley, chopped

Dust the oxtails with seasoned flour, then roast with the vegetable oil in an oven preheated to 200°C (400°F) until they begin to brown. Add the onions and when they are quite brown, the carrots, celery, leeks and turnip, and brown for another 20 minutes. Transfer all the browned ingredients to a pan, cover with the boiling veal stock, bring back to the boil and skim. Add the tomatoes, bay leaves, salt and pepper, and cook slowly for approximately 3 hours or until the meat is falling off the bone.

Let the cooked soup cool slightly, then carefully skim the fat off the surface. A lot of fat will come out of this soup so take the time to skim it thoroughly. Strain the soup into a clean pan through a conical strainer, discarding the vegetables. Take the meat off the bones and return it to the soup. Pour in the stout and return the soup to the boil. Serve over the tomatoes, then sprinkle with parsley.

BEAN AND PROSCIUTTO SOUP WITH PUMPKIN DUMPLINGS

This is a soup that uses all the spring beans, broad beans, borlotti beans, runners and butter beans, as well as fresh green peas. To make this dish you will have to ask your friendly delicatessen for a left over prosciutto bone. It will need a little meat still left on it.

The dumplings are more like the south German spaetzle than the more traditional flour and egg, or flour, potato and egg. They are dropped into the soup through a spaetzle sieve in the last 2–3 minutes of cooking.

Serve this soup on chopped tomatoes with a splash of olive oil and some grated Parmesan. Also, add some of the ubiquitous chopped parsley.

SERVES 8–10

THE SOUP

prosciutto bone	*200 g (7 oz) green and butter beans, sliced to*
50 g (2 oz) butter	*fit easily onto a soup spoon*
1 small leek, finely chopped	*300 g (11 oz) broad beans, shelled*
1 large onion, finely chopped	*200 g (7 oz) fresh peas*
300 g (11 oz) fresh borlotti beans, shelled	*1.5 L (2½ pts) Veal Stock (see page 22)*
	salt and pepper, to taste

Saute the prosciutto bone in the butter, add the leek and onion, beans and peas, and saute for a further 2 minutes. Add the hot veal stock, bring to the boil and then simmer for 50 minutes.

THE PUMPKIN DUMPLINGS

250 g (9 oz) pumpkin	*100 g (4 oz) plain flour*
1 egg	*75 g (3 oz) Parmesan cheese*
	salt and pepper, to taste

To make the dumplings, bake the pumpkin in an oven preheated to 200°C (400°F) until it is cooked and brown, then peel, remove the seeds and chop roughly. (Baking enhances the flavour, giving it a slightly caramelised taste.) Sieve and cool.

Meanwhile, beat the egg, then combine all the dumpling ingredients until just mixed. The batter should just run through the holes of the spaetzle sieve or a perforated spoon. If it is too soft, add more flour; if too firm, add a bit more beaten egg.

Remove the prosciutto bone from the soup and when it is cool enough to handle, take the meat from the bone and return the meat only to the soup. Push the dumpling batter through the sieve or perforated spoon into the soup. Simmer for 2 or 3 more minutes until they float, then serve the soup.

THE GARNISH
1 medium tomato, peeled, seeded and chopped
½ bunch parsley, chopped

150 g (5 oz) Parmesan, grated
200 ml (7 fl oz) extra virgin olive oil

To serve, stir the chopped tomato through the soup and sprinkle the parsley over it. The Parmesan and olive oil are served on the side.

CHICKEN SOUP WITH MATZOH BALL

Served with noodles this is a traditional Jewish deli dish. The matzoh ball, about the size of a large squash ball, but preferably not the same texture or colour, is made with matzoh meal, the crushed unleavened bread eaten during the Jewish feast of Passover. Made with minced chicken and melted butter, this is a slightly more indulgent version of the traditional matzoh ball.

SERVES 8
THE SOUP
1 kg (2 lb 3 oz) chicken
2 medium onions, roughly chopped
1 medium leek, roughly chopped
2 medium carrots, roughly chopped
2 sticks celery, roughly chopped

1 bulb of celeriac, roughly chopped
3 bay leaves
300 ml (11 fl oz) sherry
2.3 L (4 pts) water
salt and pepper, to taste
½ bunch parsley stalks

Put the chicken in cold water and bring it to the boil, then discard the water. Wash the pot and add all the ingredients except the parsley, seasoning well. Simmer slowly for about 2 hours, skimming constantly.

Add the parsley stalks and simmer for another 10 minutes, then strain the soup carefully through a wet napkin. The soup should be quite clear without having to clarify it.

THE BALLS
225 g (8 oz) matzoh meal
125 ml (4 oz) boiling water
1 egg, beaten

2 tablespoons butter, melted
½ bunch parsley, chopped
175 g (6 oz) chicken thigh meat, minced
salt and pepper, to taste

Cover the matzoh meal with the boiling water, allow to cool slightly. Add the egg, melted butter, parsley and minced chicken to the soaked matzoh meal, and season to taste. Divide into 8–10 pieces. Form the mix into balls and poach in the simmering soup for 15 minutes or so.

Bayswater Brasserie Book of Food

CHILLED SEAFOOD CHOWDER

This is a very versatile dish as the components can be separated and served individually. Combined, it can be served for a summer lunch or a dinner starter. For lunch, serve a large bowl with some robust bread and a green salad.

This chowder is a little like an Italian antipasto of octopus with marinated scallops, chopped mussels, chopped raw ocean trout and other seafood served in a clear lemony-flavoured fish stock. The fish, chopped potatoes, cubes of bread fried to a crisp brown, and chopped tomato makes it a colourful dish.

SERVES 8–10

THE OCEAN TROUT
1 tablespoon (½ oz) salt
2 tablespoons (1 oz) sugar
200 g (7 oz) ocean trout, diced

Mix the salt and sugar, and sprinkle fairly liberally over the fish. Cover and chill for a couple of hours. Drain all the liquid off the cured fish before adding it to the chowder.

THE OCTOPUSES
3 x 100 g (4 oz) octopuses cleaned and tenderised
juice of 3 oranges
200 ml (7 fl oz) Fish Stock (see page 23) or water
1 clove garlic, peeled
1 red onion, sliced
60 ml (2½ fl oz) olive oil
salt and pepper, to taste

Poach the octopuses for 10 minutes in the orange juice and stock with the clove of garlic and red onion. When cooked, remove the suckers from the tentacles and chop the octopuses into small pieces. Toss in the olive oil and some of the cooking liquid and chill. Strain and chill the rest of the cooking liquid as well.

THE SHELLFISH
350 g (12 oz) mussels, cleaned and debearded
4 small onions, chopped
1 bunch parsley, coarsely chopped
black pepper, to taste
2 bay leaves
500 ml (18 fl oz) water
350 g (12 oz) pippies, well soaked and cleaned of any sand
juice of 2 lemons
50 ml (2 fl oz) olive oil

To cook the mussels, put half the chopped onions, parsley, pepper and bay leaves into a pan with a lid, cover with water and steam, shaking the pan from side to side over a high heat until the mussels open. Remove from the heat as they open and discard any that don't. Strain and save the liquid. Repeat the same

Stuffed Tomato Tart   See page 64

Sliced Tomato with Fresh Cheese, Basil and Olives   See page 61

method for the pippies, using the remaining onions, parsley, pepper and bay leaf. Remove the fish from the shells and chop a little, then toss in lemon juice, olive oil and some reserved cooking liquid, and chill.

THE SNAPPER

200 g (7 oz) snapper fillet

juice of 2 limes

ground black pepper, to taste

salt, to taste

60 ml (2½ fl oz) olive oil

1 chilli, stem and seeds removed

Cut the snapper fillet into pieces about the same size as the cooked octopus. Marinate with lime juice, black pepper, salt, olive oil and chilli, and chill.

THE SCALLOPS

175 g (6 oz) or 16 scallops (2 per serve)

juice of 4 limes

Clean and remove the scallop roe, then marinate the scallops in the fresh lime juice and chill.

THE GARNISHES

3 large, firm and waxy potatoes, peeled and boiled

2 large tomatoes, peeled, seeded and chopped

100 ml (3½ fl oz) olive oil

½ bunch Italian parsley leaves

10 slices of stale bread, cut into small cubes

extra olive oil, for frying

Dice the cooked potatoes. Toss the chopped tomatoes in the olive oil and add the Italian parsley leaves.

Fry the bread to a golden brown in olive oil.

To assemble, drain the fish, reserving the liquid, then toss with the garnishes, except for the croutons. Just before serving, moisten the fish with the combined marinades and reserved cooking liquid. If the shellfish flavour seems too strong or the soup too thick, thin with a little clear fish stock. Serve the chowder well chilled with the croutons sprinkled over the top.

FRESH WHITE ONION SOUP WITH POPPY SEED CRACKERS

This is a spring or early summer soup for when green onions are fresh and at their best. It is very quick and easy to make, but is a very impressive dish if you take the trouble to make your own crackers and serve them in irregular, broken sheets with the soup. The crackers are less complicated to make than the finished product seems, and despite the miracle of modern packaging, there is no cracker as fresh and crisp as the one you have just cooked. Serve them on the side, or spread with creamy Gippsland blue cheese or mascarpone and drop them into the soup.

SERVES 8–10

THE CRACKERS

175 g (6 oz) plain flour

pinch of salt

pinch of sugar

1 tablespoon (½ oz) sesame seeds

1 tablespoon (½ oz) poppy seeds

25 g (1 oz) unsalted butter

1 egg

50 ml (2 fl oz) milk

1 tablespoon (½ oz) extra poppy seeds

To make the crackers, mix the dry ingredients together and rub in the butter. Lightly beat the egg and milk, and mix into the dry ingredients. Do not work the dough at all. Rest the dough overnight in the refrigerator.

Roll the dough out in thin sheets, about 1 mm (¹⁄₁₆ in) thick, and transfer to a tray lined with silicon paper. Just before baking, lightly brush each sheet with water and sprinkle with the extra poppy seeds. Bake in an oven preheated to 170°C (325°F) until they are golden brown. Transfer the sheets to a rack to cool.

Note: The dough will roll out very well in a pasta machine if you have one.

THE SOUP

1.1 kg (2½ lb) green onions, washed and chopped

150 g (5 oz) unsalted butter

1.1 L (2 pts) Chicken Stock (see page 23)

salt and pepper, to taste

200 ml (7 fl oz) double cream

Saute the onions gently in the butter until soft, but not browned. Cover with the chicken stock, bring to the boil, season with salt and pepper, and simmer for 20 minutes or until the onions are just soft. Puree the cooked mixture and transfer to a clean pan. Bring back to the boil, reduce the heat and mix in the double cream. Serve with the crackers.

Note: You can make the crackers a day or so in advance if you store them carefully in an airtight container. They are best, though, very fresh.

CHILLED BEETROOT SOUP

This simple beetroot puree is one of the Brasserie's most popular chilled soups. I encountered it for the first time at an uncle's house and it is one of those early food memories that has lingered.

Serve as a summer soup with heaps of chopped chives and a liberal spoonful of creme fraiche or cultured cream.

SERVES 8–10

THE SOUP
1.4 kg (3 lb) beetroots
10 black peppercorns
2 fresh bay leaves
2 teaspoons sea salt
150 g (5 oz) brown sugar

300 ml (11 fl oz) white wine vinegar
½ bunch shallots or spring onions, peeled
    and finely chopped
2 bunches chives, chopped
black pepper, to taste

Top and tail the beets and give them a good scrub. Cover with water, bring to the boil and simmer with the rest of the ingredients, except the shallots, chives and pepper, until the beets are tender. Depending on their size this will take about 1½ hours. Strain and retain the liquid.

When the beets are cool enough to handle, peel the skins off. Use your hands to do this, but unless you want indelible red mittens, wear rubber gloves.

Chop the beets into longish chunks and puree with the shallots in a food processor. Use 500 ml (18 fl oz) of the reserved cooking liquid to loosen the beets so the blender doesn't clog. Make sure the mixture is fairly thick. Chill well.

CREME FRAICHE
500 ml (18 fl oz) cream
15 ml (½ fl oz) buttermilk

To make the creme fraiche, heat the cream slightly to blood heat or 37°C (95°F). Add the buttermilk and keep covered in a warm place for 8–12 hours, then keep refrigerated.

Serve the finished soup with the creme fraiche, chopped chives and a generous grinding of fresh black pepper.

Note: Creme fraiche is a cousin of yoghurt or sour cream, but one with a rather more retiring disposition. The culture added to the cream only slightly sours and thickens it. This takes half a day or so to work, so make it the night before.

JERUSALEM ARTICHOKE SOUP WITH MUSSELS

The Jerusalem artichoke is not an artichoke. Nor, for that matter, does it come from Jerusalem or anywhere in cooee of the Holy Land. It is the tuber of the sunflower and it comes from central North America and Canada. How it came to be named remains a mystery, but the Spanish are credited with introducing it to Europe.

According to Waverley Root, the artichoke fell from grace when the potato was finally accepted.

Whatever the reason, the fall from grace has lasted a long time, which is a pity, since the Jerusalem artichoke has a well deserved place in the vegetable repertoire. It has a sweet, distinctive flavour and, in addition to this soup, can be served roasted in its skin or warm in a salad.

The mussels are more than just a companion to this soup. Using their cooking liquid for the stock gives them a full partnership in the finished flavour.

SERVES 8–10

THE MUSSELS
2 kg (4½ lb) mussels in the shell, cleaned and
    debearded
1 small onion
½ bunch parsley, chopped

350 ml (12 fl oz) white wine
350 ml (12 fl oz) Fish Stock (see page 23)
2 bay leaves
ground black pepper, to taste

Steam the mussels in the method given for the Chilled Seafood Chowder (see page 52). Discard the shells as well as any that have not opened, and set the cooked mussels aside in some of their cooking liquid. Retain the rest of the cooking liquid.

THE SOUP
1.2 kg (2¾ lb) Jerusalem artichokes, peeled and
    roughly sliced
100 g (4 oz) unsalted butter

200 ml (7 fl oz) Fish Stock (see page 23)
salt and pepper, to taste
a few saffron threads
125 ml (4 fl oz) double cream

To make the soup, sweat the artichokes in the butter, without colouring, for 5 minutes. Cover them with the fish stock and 1 L (1²/3 pts) mussel liquid, season, and add the saffron threads. Bring to the boil and simmer for 40 minutes or until tender.

Puree the soup in a blender with half the mussels, then push through a sieve into a clean pan. Return to the boil, check the seasoning and stir in the double cream just before serving.

The soup should be of a reasonably thick puree consistency, with several whole mussels in each bowl.

RAVIOLI WITH BONE MARROW IN SOUP

This is a hearty winter soup of veal broth flavoured with a variety of winter vegetables and garnished with slices of creamy pink bone marrow.

Ravioli is a fine example of the evolution and confusion of names of food. Originally the name was used for what we now call gnocchi and was never used to refer to anything stuffed. The proper name for filled pasta was originally tortelli, which is still used for something very similar to ravioli. The whole thing is very confusing, but it is also a very good reminder that various regional names and versions of dishes have been more enduring than the states and nations we attribute them to today.

Ravioli can be square (then some knowledgeable foodies would call them tortelli), round or like half moons. Square is more efficient, but round is more decorative and that is what we suggest for this soup.

SERVES 4–6

THE SOUP

2 small onions, peeled and diced

2 medium leeks, cleaned and diced

2 medium carrots, diced

1 bulb of celeriac, diced

2 medium turnips, diced

50 ml (2 fl oz) olive oil

1 L (1²/₃ pt) strong Veal Stock (see page 22)

4 medium tomatoes, skinned, seeded and chopped

salt and pepper, to taste

250 g (9 oz) green beans, stringed and sliced

Saute the onions, leeks, carrots, celeriac and turnips in the olive oil until they are clear and soft. Cover with the stock, add the tomatoes, season and simmer for 1½–2 hours. Add the beans in the last 5 minutes, making sure they still have some crunch.

THE RAVIOLI FILLING

12 x 6 cm (2½ in) pieces bone marrow (removed from bones)

150 g (5 oz) veal nut

150 g (5 oz) pork fat

1 tablespoon fresh marjoram leaves

100 g (4 oz) grated Parmesan cheese

salt and black pepper, to taste

Grate half the bone marrow and cut the rest in 6 mm (¼ in) slices. Chop and then finely mince the veal and pork fat.

Mix all the ingredients together except the bone marrow slices. Reserve some of the slices for the filling and the rest for the soup.

THE PASTA DOUGH

300 g (11 oz) plain flour

3 eggs

1 teaspoon salt

200 g (7 oz) medium grade semolina

Put the flour in a bowl, make a well in the centre and add the eggs and salt. Mix to form a dry dough, then roll through the rollers of a pasta machine, dusting with semolina, until it is as thin as you can make it without any holes appearing. Cut the dough into rounds and line them up in pairs along the dusted bench.

Put spoonfuls of the filling and a slice of the bone marrow onto half the rounds. Carefully brush a little water around the edges of the filled rounds, then press the remaining rounds on top, pressing down the edges to seal firmly. Experienced ravioli makers will make the seal into a decoration of crimps.

TO SERVE
200 ml (7 fl oz) extra virgin olive oil   *175 g (6 oz) freshly grated Parmesan cheese*

Bring the soup to near boiling, then put in the ravioli and the remaining sliced marrow and cook them. To serve, spoon into bowls, splash a little olive oil on top and serve with freshly grated Parmesan on the side.

RED CAPSICUM PUREE WITH SALT COD AND A POACHED EGG

This is a very handsome lunch. The bright red sweet capsicum puree, the white flakes of the fish and golden brown of the sauteed chunks of potato, topped with the creamy white and rich yellow of a perfectly poached egg, make a dazzling dish. Serve it with a chunk of crusty bread.

SERVES 8

THE COD AND POTATOES   *4 large old potatoes*
400 g (14 oz) cod (this is 1 side of cod)   *olive oil*

Soak the cod overnight in plenty of cold water, changing the water a few times if you can. Poach the fish in plain water for about 15–20 minutes. When it is cool enough to handle, skin the fish and flake the flesh from the bones. Save 750 ml (1½ pts) of the cooking liquid.

Wash the potatoes and boil them in their jackets, then peel and slice or roughly chop them. Reserve.

THE CAPSICUM PUREE   *750 ml (1½ pts) Fish Stock (see page 23)*
50 ml (2 fl oz) olive oil   *black pepper, to taste*
2 onions, roughly chopped   *8 eggs, poached (see page 38)*
1 leek, roughly chopped   *½ bunch purple basil*
1 fennel bulb, roughly chopped   *½ bunch Italian parsley*
1 kg (2 lb 3 oz) red capsicums, roughly chopped

Heat the olive oil in a pan and saute the vegetables and capsicums until soft. Cover with the fish stock and the reserved cooking liquid from the cod. Simmer for 45 minutes or until the vegetables are all cooked through, then puree and return to a clean pan. Season to taste with pepper.

Saute the cooked potatoes in olive oil until golden brown, then add, with the cod, to the puree and simmer gently for a further 15 minutes. Serve topped with a poached egg and garnished with purple basil and Italian parsley.

SLICED TOMATO WITH FRESH CHEESE, BASIL AND OLIVES

The wonderful simplicity of this dish demands the very best ingredients. There is no point in making it with anything less. Eating this salad should be an occasion to reflect on the fact that the art of great eating has nothing to do with complexity, just perfect combinations.

The tomatoes that this dish deserves will probably be the hardest ingredient to find. The beefsteak tomato, Rouge de Mamande, or Italian plum tomato are the most suitable. Choose them with care. They must be perfectly ripe (preferably sun ripened) and red, and served at room temperature. One tomato per serve ought to be enough, depending always on what else is offered with the dish. It is splendid alone but it can also be served alongside a veal scallopini or pasta dish at dinner.

A fresh soft cow's cheese, light in flavour and with the consistency of a ricotta, should be used. These cheeses are low in fat, fairly low in cholesterol and easy to digest.

The merits of olive oils are as fiercely contested as those of football teams. A basic truth is that the better the oil the better the salad. Extra virgin olive oil should be used and Colonna, from Molise in Central Italy, is one of the best.

SERVES 4

4 tomatoes

6 x 60 g (2½ oz) fresh cow's milk cheeses or
    baby mozzarellas

24 large Kalamata olives

½ bunch basil leaves, red and green, either
    shredded or picked

60 ml (2½ fl oz) extra virgin olive oil

40 ml (1½ fl oz) balsamic vinegar

sea salt and freshly ground black pepper, to taste

Slice the tomatoes into a dish and spread them in a circle. Arrange the cheese, olives and basil over the top. Sprinkle with olive oil, balsamic vinegar, sea salt and pepper.

Drink something very robust but fresh to the palate with this.

ROASTED VEGETABLE SALAD WITH TWICE FRIED BEANS

R oasted vegetables have a very special flavour and you can influence this by what you add to the roasting dish. In this dish the vegetables are roasted in a good olive oil with a handful of rosemary and fresh bay leaves tossed in at the end, but you can experiment with other fresh herbs. Try roasting extra vegetables with a dinner meat dish and setting them aside for a lunch time salad the next day.

This dish is better at room temperature rather than cold.

The beans are fried twice, the first time to blister the skin and the second to cook them through. The toasted sunflower kernels add crunch to the finished dish.

SERVES 4–6

THE MARINADE FOR THE BEANS

50 ml (2 fl oz) soy sauce

300 ml (11 fl oz) Chicken Stock (see page 23) or water

1 teaspoon sesame oil

1 piece of ginger root, grated

zest of 2 lemons

Combine all the marinade ingredients and leave for the flavours to develop.

THE BEANS AND SALAD

4 tablespoons sunflower kernels

2 tablespoons soy sauce

2 L (3½ pts) grape seed oil

175 g (6 oz) green beans, stringed

175 (6 oz) butter beans, stringed

1 bunch rocket leaves, washed and dried

½ bunch watercress leaves, washed and dried

50 ml (2 fl oz) vinaigrette

Lightly sprinkle the sunflower kernels with soy sauce, then toast in an oven preheated to 140°C (275°F). Roast, moving the kernels during cooking to coat thoroughly with sauce, until the sauce has completely evaporated. Let them dry on a hot tray.

Heat the oil in a deep fryer until almost smoking hot, then quickly fry the beans twice, making sure they do not lose their bright colour during the second frying. Drain them and add them to the marinade.

THE ROAST VEGETABLES

8 baby carrots

1 small daikon (Japanese white radish)

8 baby turnips

4 small potatoes

8 small squash

4 small yellow zucchini

150 ml (5 fl oz) olive oil

salt and pepper, to taste

4 sprigs of rosemary

2 fresh bay leaves

Wash and peel the vegetables if necessary, keeping them as intact as possible. Heat the olive oil in a roasting pan on top of the stove, season the vegetables, and brown them all except the zucchini. Roast the browned vegetables in an oven preheated to 180°C (350°F) until tender, adding the zucchini for the last 10–15 minutes. About 5 minutes or so before the end of cooking, throw in the rosemary and bay leaves. If you are reheating already roasted vegetables, put the herbs in for most of the cooking time. Leave to cool just until warm.

To serve, sprinkle the root vegetables with the vinaigrette, and toss with the rocket and cress leaves. Arrange the vegetables and leaves on each plate, pile the beans on top and sprinkle with the sunflower kernels.

BLUE MOUNTAIN MUSHROOMS, PICKLED GOLDEN SHALLOTS AND PANCETTA

In the last few years people have been gathering edible wild mushrooms around Sydney, in the Blue Mountains particularly. They are usually found in introduced habitats like lawns or pine forests, so they are not native. There are at least three or four edible varieties, but if you are going to collect them do a thorough course in mushroom spotting. Some fungi are not at all friendly to the human metabolism.

The species in this dish are not, of course, endemic to the Blue Mountains, but that is where the Bayswater Brasserie first got them from, and in any case, an aura of romance clings to it so Blue Mountain they will remain. They are more properly known as Saffron Milk Caps, which some may find romantic, but to me seems clumsy and confused. It is a variety also found in France, where in Normandy it is called Orange and in Provence, Sanguine.

Bacon is a traditional friend of the mushroom, and the Italian cured pork, pancetta, used in this dish comes from the same part of the pig, but it has a much more sophisticated and subtle flavour.

SERVES 4–6

THE PICKLED SHALLOTS (enough for 2 mushroom recipes)
300 g (11 oz) Golden Shallots
140 ml (4½ fl oz) white wine vinegar

50 g (2 oz) caster sugar
1 teaspoon freshly grated horseradish
4–5 threads of saffron

Peel the shallots by pouring a small amount of boiling water over and letting them stand for a couple of minutes to loosen the skin. Bring all the other ingredients to the boil and pour over the shallots. Store in jars for at least 3 weeks before using.

THE MUSHROOMS
100 g (4 oz) piece pancetta
16 medium Saffron Milk Caps, cleaned
750 ml (25 fl oz) Chicken Stock (see page 23)

½ bunch parsley, picked and chopped (save the stalks)
75 g (3 oz) unsalted butter
50 g (2 oz) unsalted butter, cold and chopped

Remove the skin from the pancetta and cover with cold water. Bring to the boil and simmer for 2 minutes, then remove, and when cool enough to handle, slice it as thinly as possible. Lay the slices on kitchen paper on a baking tray and bake in an oven preheated to 180°C (350°F) until they are crisp. Set aside in a warm place.

Cover the mushrooms with the chicken stock and parsley stalks. Bring to the boil and simmer for 10–12 minutes, drain the mushrooms and reduce the stock to 200 ml (7 fl oz).

Melt the 75 g (3 oz) butter in a large heavy-based frying pan and heat until it foams. Slice the pickled shallots and saute them in the butter until golden brown. Add two tablespoons of vinegar from the pickle and 200 ml (7 fl oz) of the chicken stock to the frying pan and bring to the boil. Whisk the cold butter through the stock, vinegar and shallots to emulsify.

To serve, place the drained mushrooms on a plate and ladle the shallots and sauce over. Scatter the pancetta slices and chopped parsley on top.

STUFFED TOMATO TART

This dish is a pleasant combination of ideas, a kind of flaky pastry raft with a cargo of stuffed tomatoes sitting in a custard. The effect can be entirely spoiled, however, if you do not let the tomatoes drain, as they are likely to turn the raft into a soggy slab.

SERVES 8
THE TART
300 g (11 oz) puff pastry

Line a 23 cm (9 in) flan ring and cook the base blind as on page 35.

THE FILLING
8 medium-sized ripe tomatoes
1 teaspoon sea salt
4 tablespoons unsalted butter
6 peeled shallots, chopped

400 g (14 oz) mushrooms, sliced
salt and pepper, to taste
4 tablespoons soft breadcrumbs
6 eggs
300 ml (11 fl oz) cream

Core the tomatoes and, if you are using the blanching method to peel them, make a cross on the other side with a sharp knife, and plunge them into boiling water for 10 seconds. Refresh them in iced water. Remove the skins and cut off each top to make a lid. Scoop out the seeds and the pulp. Sprinkle the hollowed tomatoes and lids with sea salt and set aside for 40 minutes to drain.

Heat the butter in a pan and saute the shallots until they are tender. Add the mushrooms, season, and cook for another 5 minutes. Add the breadcrumbs and mix together well to make the stuffing.

Carefully dry and drain off any liquid from inside the tomatoes. Spoon in the stuffing. Put the tops on and sit on a rack covered with a cloth to dry.

Beat together the eggs and cream, and season.

Arrange the tomatoes on the pastry base so that when serving the tart you slice through their centres. Pour the egg and cream mix around the tomatoes and bake in an oven preheated to 220°C (425°F) for 10 minutes. Reduce the heat to 180°C (350°F) and cook until the custard is set. This will take another 45 minutes or so. Serve the tart with a crisp green salad.

PIZZA OF VARIOUS KINDS

The pizza is the archetypal lunch, a kind of edible plate capable of supporting all kinds of delicious meats and savoury flavours or, if simplicity is your measure of culinary joy, just a very satisfactory combination of tomato and cheese.

The panache and equipment of the commercial pizza maker suggests that this, like most apparently simple dishes, is a formidable undertaking. In fact, it is basically quite simple, but unless you have an oven that will reach 300°C (600°F) or thereabouts—quite a bit beyond the normal domestic range—you might find making the right kind of base elusive.

If by chance you can reach that temperature, your oven can be quite simply converted to a pizza oven by adding a ceramic kiln shelf to the hottest part. The shelf, which you can buy from a craft supplier, should be about 10 cm (4 in) smaller all round than the oven floor. It radiates the oven heat up through the pizza dough so it cooks through crisply from both top and bottom, giving the bottom its distinctive hard surface while letting the top of the dough take up all the flavours.

Because the pizza is such a splendid lunch dish, along with its sibling, the *calzoni*, and foreign cousin, the *fougasse*, we offer the recipe just in case your oven is up to it.

The dough for all three leavened breads is the same. This quantity will make 8 pizzas or fougasse, or 6 calzoni.

SERVES 6

THE BASIC PIZZA

450 g (16 oz) plain flour

a large pinch of salt

25 g (1 oz) yeast

300 ml (11 fl oz) water

On the workbench, make a mound of the flour and salt with a well in the centre. Break the yeast into the well, add the water and mix, then knead until perfectly smooth. Then put this dough in a bowl, covering the bowl with a damp cloth, and set it aside in a warm place to let it prove until doubled in size.

This will take about 1 hour and you can fill in the time by finishing the Onion Puree (see page 128). This takes about 2 hours so you should have it well on the way before you start making the dough.

Tip the risen dough onto the bench and knead it again for a moment to knock the air out of it. Cut it into six pieces and, on a well floured board, roll each out to a flat round about 3 mm (⅛ in) thick and spread with onion puree. Arrange the topping.

Bake in an oven preheated to 300°C (600°F) for about 8 minutes, moving the base about on the hot ceramic shelf. Sprinkle the cooked pizza with a little more oil and fresh herbs, and serve.

PIZZA TOPPING

KING PRAWNS AND CHILLI OIL

Strong flavours are preferable on a pizza and excessive amounts of toppings should be avoided; piles of cheese and tomato for instance makes a soggy base. In the best pizzas the topping and bread base are equal partners in the finished dish. In the worst pizzas, the base is reduced to a necessary boredom.

Seafood is a fine pizza topping and king prawns or large harbour prawns are ideal. I prefer the latter, but it really is a matter of personal taste and what is available.

SERVES 6

THE PRAWNS

*3–4 medium king prawns per serve, shelled
    and washed*

50 ml (2 fl oz) chilli oil

black pepper, to taste

grated zest of 2 lemons

1 recipe Pizza Dough (see page 66)

100 g (4 oz) Onion Puree (see page 128)

*3 large tomatoes, peeled, seeded, chopped and
    well drained*

24 dried tomatoes

100 ml (3½ fl oz) each of chilli oil and olive oil

125 g (4½ oz) Parmesan cheese, freshly grated

1 bunch basil leaves, chopped

Marinate the prawns in the 50 ml (2 fl oz) chilli oil, the black pepper and the lemon zest.

Roll the pizza dough into 6 circles 3 mm (⅛ in) thick and brush with the onion puree. Put the chopped and dried tomatoes on top of the pizza bases, then arrange the prawns on top of the dried tomatoes to prevent them drying out during cooking. A bit of commonsense is a great help when you are constructing your pizza. Things like the tomatoes or slices of dried sausage, for instance, need some care to survive the heat. Sprinkle with chilli oil to taste, Parmesan cheese and the olive oil, and slide into an oven preheated to 300°C (600°F) for 8 minutes.

Sprinkle the cooked pizzas with a little more of both oils and the chopped basil leaves.

PIZZA TOPPING

DUCK SAUSAGE PIZZA AND GRILLED RED CAPSICUMS

Both hot and sweet sausages are traditional pizza meats. The most commonly used sweet sausage is the Italian, with fennel seeds, pepper and garlic. The hot version has chilli flakes and paprika added to give it a red colour. You can also use pancetta—the unsmoked bacon—prosciutto, salami or pepperoni. In Lancashire, no doubt, they even use black pudding.

Some sausages, like the duck sausages in this dish, will need precooking.

SERVES 6

6 x 100 g (4 oz) Duck Sausages (see page 26)
1 recipe Pizza Dough (see page 66)
100 g (4 oz) Onion Puree (see page 128)
2 large tomatoes, peeled, seeded, chopped and well drained
3 large red capsicums, grilled, peeled and cut into strips

30 black or green olives, pitted
200 g (7 oz) stracchino, cut into strips
2 small bunches sage leaves
50 ml (2 fl oz) chilli oil
50 ml (2 fl oz) olive oil
freshly ground black pepper

Place the duck sausages in a covered pan of cold water and bring them to the boil, set aside to cool, then slice.

Roll out the pizza bases at this point and brush with onion puree. Arrange the chopped tomatoes, sausage slices, capsicum strips, olives and stracchino on top of the bases. Sprinkle with fresh sage leaves, chilli and olive oils, and lots of black pepper. Slide into an oven preheated to 300°C (600°F) and bake for 8 minutes or until well browned and crisp.

CALZONI WITH FOUR CHEESES AND OLIVE PUREE

The calzoni was no doubt invented by some ingenious diner who was looking for a transportable pizza, and that is what it is. The round of pizza dough is folded over the filling like a half moon and then baked. A smaller version, *calzuneddi*, comes from Apulia where it is deep fried in olive oil to make a delicious snack. Elsewhere this minature calzoni is called *panzarotti*.

The meaning of calzoni is "pant legs" and the dish is supposed to resemble the baggy trousers that Neapolitan men once wore. In some parts of Italy the calzoni is called *mezzaluna* or half moon which, just to add to the confusion, is also the name of a curved chopping knife, so when ordering it in Italy stick to the first version.

Ideally, the full sized calzoni needs much the same heat as a pizza, but you can get away with less if you make the dough a little thicker and bake it longer. You will need to have your oven on its highest setting and the kiln shelf will have to be buzzing.

SERVES 6

1 recipe Pizza Dough (see page 66)
100 g (4 oz) grated Parmesan cheese
100 g (4 oz) grated stracchino
100 g (4 oz) Fromage Fermier goat's cheese
100 g (4 oz) ricotta cheese
2 small tomatoes, peeled, seeded, chopped and
*   well drained*

4 tablespoons Olive Puree
225 g (8 oz) oyster mushrooms, dry-fried
*   until brown*
½ bunch each red and green basil leaves
50 ml (2 fl oz) olive oil
sea salt and pepper, to taste
50 g (2 oz) extra Parmesan cheese, grated

Divide the dough into six pieces and roll these into balls. Dust them with a little flour and roll each ball out into a 3 mm (⅛ in) thick circle. Stretch the dough slightly so that it becomes elongated, then slide onto a well floured pizza peel or fish slice. (The calzoni are cooked directly on a baking tray or kiln shelf.)

In the centre of each calzoni, spoon a tablespoon of each cheese and the chopped tomato, a couple of teaspoons of the olive puree, a small pile of the mushrooms and a generous amount of the basil leaves. Reserve some of the basil. Fold the dough over, as you would an apple turnover, and with floured fingers, press the edges of the dough firmly together, making sure it is well sealed. Do not moisten either the underside of the calzoni or the pizza peel.

Brush each completed half moon with olive oil and sprinkle with the sea salt, pepper and Parmesan. Place a few basil leaves on top and, if you like, dot the calzoni with a few small pieces of fairly dry chopped tomato. Bake in an oven preheated to 260°C (500°F) for about 10 minutes.

PEPPER PAPPARDELLE, DUCK SAUSAGE AND BASIL

Pappardelle are long flat noodles which are traditionally served in the Tuscan region during the game season. One of the most famous dishes they appear in is with a hare sauce. The hare is cooked with vegetables and red wine to make the sauce, but the meat is not used in the dish.

In this dish, freshly ground or cracked black pepper has been added to the pasta dough, but any other ground spices could also be used. If you decide to make your own duck sausages, then make them in advance and let them hang in the refrigerator at least overnight to dry. If they are too fresh when cooked, they tend to split.

SERVES 6

THE PASTA DOUGH
500 g (18 oz) plain flour
1 teaspoon salt

50 g (2 oz) freshly ground black pepper (very fine)
4 eggs

Put the flour and seasoning in a bowl, make a well in the centre, add the 4 eggs and mix to a firm dry dough. Roll it out in a pasta machine until fine enough to pass through the rollers when set on the last notch. Once the pasta has been rolled down, dust with flour, fold it over lengthways and cut into 3–4 cm (1½ in) wide strips with a knife or a pastry wheel.

THE SAUSAGE AND THE SAUCE
6 x 100 g (4 oz) Duck Sausages (see page 26)
50 ml (2 fl oz) olive oil
150 ml (5 fl oz) white wine
225 ml (8 fl oz) Duck Stock (see page 23)

½ bunch basil leaves
3 medium tomatoes, peeled, chopped and seeded
75 g (3 oz) unsalted butter, cold and chopped
150 g (5 oz) black olives
salt and pepper, to taste

To cook the duck sausages prick them, cover with cold water and bring them to the boil, then drain and slice.

Heat a little olive oil in a heavy-based pan and saute the sliced sausages until brown. Remove and keep them warm. Add the white wine to the oil and sausage juices, and reduce until it has almost evaporated. Add the duck stock, basil leaves and chopped tomato, then whisk in the cold butter. Return the sausage to the pan, add the black olives, warm quickly and take the pan off the heat.

Blanch the pappardelle in a large pan of boiling salted water for a minute or so. Toss the noodles in the sauce, return the sauce to the boil, check the seasoning and serve in a pasta bowl.

Note: Make sure the pepper used in the pasta dough is very finely ground or it will make holes in the dough when rolling.

FOUGASSE WITH FOUR STYLES OF MARINATED FISH

Fougasse, fouace or fouasse is a kind of French cousin to the pizza. Larousse describes it as one of the oldest of French pastries, but if it had the same genesis as almost everything else in French cuisine, it might actually have travelled to France from Italy.

There are, though, some major differences between the French and Italian usages of this flat leavened bread. The good news is that this one does not require the same fierce heat that a pizza base does, so it is easily cooked in the domestic oven. Originally it was cooked under the cinders of the hearth. It is thicker than the pizza and is not usually served *under* something, but more often in or alongside things. Fougasse can be baked in advance, but a crunchy crispness is the essence of this bread, so do not refrigerate.

At the Brasserie it is sometimes served with a braised lamb shank and baby turnips, a vegetable casserole, or with soup. This dish with four styles of marinated fish, is a well established Bayswater favourite.

SERVES 4–6

THE FOUGASSE
1 recipe Pizza Dough (see page 66)
1 recipe Onion Puree (see page 128)

sea salt and ground black pepper, to taste
chopped herbs, to taste
olive oil, to taste

To make the fougasse, roll out the dough to a 1 cm (½ in) thickness. Cut 4 holes in each piece, then stretch it slightly by hand. Brush with onion puree, season to taste and sprinkle with the herbs and olive oil. Leave in a warm place for 20 minutes to complete rising, then bake on a kiln shelf or baking tray in an oven preheated to 250°C (500°F) for 10–12 minutes.

THE OCEAN TROUT
200 g (7 oz) ocean trout

1 tablespoon sea salt
2 tablespoons caster sugar

Cut the trout into 8 slices and spread them out on a tray. Sprinkle a mixture of the salt and sugar evenly over them and chill for 2–3 hours to cure. Before serving, wipe each slice free of the salt and sugar, and any brine that has formed.

THE RED MULLET
4 very small red mullet, about 50 g (2 oz) each
1 small red onion, sliced
1 red capsicum, grilled, peeled and cut into strips
1 red chilli, split and seeded

1 teaspoon grated horseradish
4 fresh bay leaves
½ bunch basil, coarsely chopped
150 ml (5 fl oz) white wine vinegar
50 g (2 oz) sugar

Carefully fillet the mullet and remove the bones, leaving the skin on. Slice the

Steamed Choy Sum with Shredded Duck and Egg   See page 85

Saffron Noodles, Cured Ocean Trout and Olive Puree See page 73

onion, then layer the mullet, onion and capsicums in a dish and cover them with the remaining ingredients. Leave at room temperature to marinate for 2–3 hours.

THE SARDINES
8 fresh sardines
30 ml (1 fl oz) olive oil
1 clove garlic, peeled and chopped
3 red chillies, split and seeded
1 small onion, chopped
1 teaspoon ground paprika

1 teaspoon ground black pepper
1 teaspoon ground cummin seeds
1 teaspoon ground coriander seeds
¼ teaspoon saffron powder
100 ml (3½ fl oz) red wine vinegar
½ bunch coriander leaves
½ bunch Italian parsley leaves

To prepare the sardines, scale and gut them, then slit around the back of the head. Holding the head, carefully pull out the backbone and ribs, trying to keep the flesh and skin intact. Break the backbone off at the tail. Keep the flesh and skin, whole if possible, set in a dish.

Heat the oil in a pan and fry the garlic, chillies and onion until they are golden brown. Add all the spices and continue to fry gently until they are toasted. Add the vinegar and bring to the boil. Remove from the heat and add the coriander and parsley leaves. Let this cool just until warm, then pour over the sardines.

THE GARFISH
4 garfish, filletted and skinned
juice of 2 limes

Cover the garfish fillets with a damp cloth and just before serving, cut each fillet into 3 and squeeze over the lime juice.

To serve the whole dish, arrange a selection of fish on each plate with the fougasse on the side.

SAFFRON NOODLES, CURED OCEAN TROUT AND OLIVE PUREE

This is one of my favourite noodle dishes; a view shared by Brasserie patrons who have consumed it in increasing quantities since it first appeared on the menu.

It is a delightfully simple dish to prepare and extremely attractive with a combination of golden noodles, pink chunks of ocean trout, bright red chopped tomatoes and reddish-black olive puree.

The olive puree—olive pulp mixed with extra virgin olive oil—can be bought ready made. On its own, it makes a wonderful supper dish spread on hot toast.

SERVES 4–6

THE OCEAN TROUT

500 g (18 oz) piece ocean trout, cut from
  the fillet

25 g (1 oz) sea salt

50 g (2 oz) sugar

Make sure the fillet is completely free of small bones and chop it into 1 cm
(½ in) squares. Cure it with the salt and sugar, and refrigerate. If you are going
to keep it longer than 2–3 hours, pour off the accumulated brine.

THE SAFFRON NOODLES

500 g (18 oz) plain flour

½ teaspoon salt

½ teaspoon saffron threads, ground to powder
  in a mortar

3 eggs

200 g (7 oz) medium grade semolina,
  for dusting

4 medium tomatoes, peeled, seeded and chopped

2 tablespoons olive puree (Benza Lupi)

To make the pasta, mix the flour, salt and saffron powder in a cake mixer fitted
with a dough hook, and add 2 of the eggs. Mix, do not knead, the kneading
is done by the pasta machine rollers. If it seems too dry mix in the other egg
a bit at a time. The dough should form a firm, smooth ball. Roll the dough
through the machine down to the number one notch a couple of times, then cut
into noodles with the fine cutter. Use the semolina for dusting the dough and
the finished noodles.

To cook the noodles, blanch them for a ½–1 minute in boiling salted water,
then drain and toss in a heavy-based frying pan of foaming butter.

Serve the noodles mounded in a bowl, topped with the ocean trout with
some of its juice, the chopped tomato with some of its juice, and the olive puree.

INK NOODLES AND VERMICELLI, CUTTLEFISH AND LEMON

This is another simple and very attractive noodle dish. The combination
of the blackish ink noodles and the white vermicelli looks very attractive.
The contrast of flavours and textures of the two is also very satisfying.

SERVES 4–6

THE CUTTLEFISH

6 x 120 g (4½ oz) cuttlefish

100 g (4 oz) unsalted butter

juice of ½ a lemon

freshly ground black pepper, to taste

a small glass of Japanese sake

½ bunch Italian parsley

Bone the cuttlefish. Remove the ink sacs and reserve for the noodles. Remove
the tentacles and the beak, then skin and slice the body, and set the pieces aside.

THE INK NOODLES AND THE VERMICELLI
225 g (8 oz) plain flour
1 tablespoon gluten flour
½ teaspoon salt

2 eggs
200 g (7 oz) medium grade semolina,
  for dusting
¼ packet Chinese dried rice noodles

Cover the reserved ink sacs with water, bring to the boil and strain. Set aside to cool.

To make the pasta, mix the flour, salt and eggs in a cake mixer fitted with a dough hook, and add 2 tablespoons of cuttlefish ink to make a firm, smooth dough. Roll the dough through the pasta machine until smooth and very thin, then cut into noodles.

Heat the butter until foaming in a heavy-based frying pan and lightly saute the cuttlefish pieces for not more than 30 seconds, adding the lemon juice, black pepper and sake at the end.

Blanch the noodles and vermicelli together for 30 seconds in a large pan of boiling, salted water. Drain, then transfer them to the pan with the cuttlefish, and toss in the hot juice. Serve garnished with the Italian parsley.

CHICKEN AND POTATO PIE

The pie must rank along with the wheel as one of humankind's most amazing inventions. A delicious meal, savoury or sweet, with fruit, fish, vegetable, meat or fowl cooked inside a crunchy and edible container.

In modern times the commercially manufactured pie with its gloomy and glutenous mysteries has given the species a bad name. Pies deserve better than that.

This pie, some extreme purists might argue, is more in the nature of a pasty, since the crust is all enfolding like a Beef Wellington and the lid and case are not distinct entities. It is designed to be sliced and served warm, with a simple green salad supported, if you like, with toasted walnuts, or is delicious moistened with the tomato sauce given here.

SERVES 6–8

THE PIE
8 small chicken breasts, skinned and shredded
4 small potatoes, peeled and sliced as thinly as
  possible
2 cloves garlic, chopped
2 small onions, peeled and chopped

½ bunch fresh sage, chopped
salt and black pepper, to taste
500 g (18 oz) puff pastry
milk or beaten egg, for glazing
2 eggs
200 ml (7 fl oz) cream

Mix the chicken, potatoes, garlic, onion and sage together well, then season with salt and pepper.

Roll the pastry into a 40 x 25 cm (16 x 10 in) rectangle about 3 mm (⅛ in) thick. Lay the mixed filling down one side and fold it over like a giant apple turnover. Press the edges together making a firm seal and turn the pie over so the join is underneath. Make a small hole in the top about the size of a 20 cent piece. Brush the pastry with a little milk or beaten egg, then bake in an oven preheated to 180°C (350°F) for 20 minutes.

Whisk the eggs and cream together without mixing too much air into them. Take the pie from the oven and pour this mixture into the hole, being careful to disperse it evenly throughout the inside of the pie. Reduce the heat to 180°C (350°F) and bake for another 25 minutes.

THE TOMATO SAUCE
75 ml (3 fl oz) olive oil

6 medium tomatoes, halved
salt and pepper, to taste

Heat the oil in a saucepan. Season the tomatoes with the salt and pepper, then cook until they are completely soft. Puree the tomatoes and return to a clean pan. Check the seasoning and bring it back to the boil. The sauce should be on the thick side, so if it seems too thin cook until reduced to the right consistency.

Let the pie rest on a cooling rack for a good 15 minutes after cooking, then serve in wide slices on top of the sauce.

GNOCCHI WITH TOMATO SAUCE AND BASIL

One great Italian gastronomic guide lists no less than twelve different gnocchi and every Italian region has at least one distinctive version. Mostly they are made with potato, but they can also be made with choux pastry, polenta or pumpkin.

Like most simple dishes, it requires more than a little skill and judgement to make well. The secret is to make them light enough, yet strong enough to stay together while cooking. Gnocchi can be served in a wonderful variety of ways, with creamy sauce, with melted butter and grated Parmesan in soups, and in stews. At the Brasserie I have served them with a delicious cream sauce of fresh green beans and Gippsland blue cheese. The dish given here, though, is a favourite.

SERVES 4
THE TOMATO SAUCE
100 ml (3½ fl oz) olive oil
2 small onions, peeled and finely chopped

800 g (1¾ lb) ripe Italian plum tomatoes
salt and pepper, to taste
1 bunch basil leaves

Heat the oil in a saucepan and saute the onions until they are clear and soft. Add the tomatoes, season with salt and pepper, and simmer over a low heat for 20–30 minutes. Add the basil leaves at the end and pass the mixture through a fine food mill or puree in a blender.

THE GNOCCHI
500 g (18 oz) old waxy potatoes
125 g (4 oz) plain flour
100 g (4 oz) grated Parmesan cheese
a couple of grinds of nutmeg

1 teaspoon salt
freshly ground white pepper
½ a beaten egg
200 g (7 oz) extra flour, for dusting

Choose your potatoes with care; old and waxy are the best, old and floury will do, new and floury are a dead loss. Cook the potatoes in their skins in salted water, then peel them and pass through a fine mouli or sieve.

Put the potatoes and all dry ingredients on a floured board, make a well in the centre and mix in the beaten egg. Do not knead the mix too vigorously or it will become very sticky and glutenous. Separate the dough into 8 pieces and roll each by hand into lengths about 1 cm (⅜ in) in diameter. Make sure there is plenty of flour on the gnocchi, then cut each length into 4 cm (1½ in) long pieces. If preferred, give them a distinctive shape by pressing each with a fork. Slide them onto floured kitchen paper and leave until you are going to cook them.

Slide the gnocchi into a pan of rapidly boiling, salted water. The gnocchi are cooked when they float to the surface. Lift them out with a wire mesh spoon, straight into the reheated tomato sauce. Serve in pasta bowls accompanied by extra Parmesan cheese and cracked black pepper.

DEEP-FRIED SMALL FISH WITH VIETNAMESE MINT AND VINEGAR DRESSING

Any number of small fish can be used for this dish—red mullet, red spot whiting, garfish, sardines, leatherjackets or creamfish. The greater the variety the more attractive the dish.

The fish are scaled, gutted and deep fried with the heads on or off, according to your taste. We like them on. For frying, use a proper frying vessel of thin pressed steel with a wire basket.

The oil or fat you use is also a matter of taste. Personally we think it is an aesthetic mistake to use animal fats or lard for frying anything, let alone fish. Olive oil has a low smoke point and therefore a tendency to become acrid, while peanut oil has a high flash point so is good for frying, but it can be a bit too heavy in flavour. Grape seed is ideal. So when we say the choice of medium is a matter of taste, we actually mean exercise your good taste and use grape seed oil!

The oil should be at 180°C (350°F) for frying so it's a good idea to check with a thermometer. In deep frying it is important that the temperature is regained as quickly as possible after the food is put in. The food needs to be surrounded by plenty of hot oil, so do not try to cook too much at one time and try to put in a few fish of approximately the same size in each batch.

SERVES 4

THE FISH

8 small garfish, gutted and scaled

12 small red mullet, scaled only

4 small sardines, gutted and scaled

flour, seasoned with salt and pepper

oil for deep frying

Dredge the fish in the seasoned flour and deep fry them until they are crisp.

THE DRESSING

150 ml (5 fl oz) rice vinegar

50 ml (2 fl oz) thick soy sauce

150 ml (5 fl oz) fish sauce (Nom Pla)

250 ml (9 fl oz) water

6 bunches Vietnamese mint, picked

juice and zest of 2 limes

2 small red chillies, seeded and chopped

Whisk the rice vinegar, soy sauce and fish sauce together with the water, then mix with the mint, juice and chillies. Since lime juice soon loses its distinctive flavour after being exposed to air, and might then just as well be lemon, do not squeeze the limes or grate the zest in advance. Only add immediately before serving .

Ladle the vinegar dressing onto the plates, with plenty of mint leaves, then lay the crisp fish on top.

BARBECUED OCTOPUS WITH VARIOUS COMPLEMENTS

This is an immense favourite with Brasserie regulars and if we ever wanted to take it off the menu there would be more than a few sullen customers. Along with the Thai Chicken Curry, this dish is likely to be around for a long time.

The local fish market that supplies the Brasserie tenderise their small octopuses by whirling them around in a concrete mixer for a couple of hours. Octopuses can be a tough proposition if they haven't had some kind of preparation, so if you do not have a concrete mixer in your kitchen, remove the heads and beaks, put the octopuses in a stout plastic bag and pound them flat with a wooden mallet.

These can be served on their own, with a simple salad of dressed garden leaves, or with any of the following more robust complements.

Lunch

SERVES 4

THE OCTOPUSES

12 x 50 g (2 oz) small octopuses, cleaned
olive oil

juice of 6 limes
ground black pepper

To prepare the octopuses, brush with olive oil and add a squeeze of lime juice
and a sprinkling of black pepper. Barbecue quickly on the char-grill or until the
edges are crispy and the thicker parts are pink and soft.

RATATOUILLE

8 very small eggplants
1 tablespoon sea salt
50 ml (2 fl oz) olive oil
1 clove garlic, peeled
4 small yellow zucchini, cut into batons

4 small green zucchini, cut into batons
salt and pepper, to taste
4 small tomatoes, peeled, seeded and quartered
½ bunch Italian parsley, chopped
½ bunch fresh oregano, chopped

To prepare the ratatouille, halve the eggplants and sprinkle them with salt. Let
them stand until the salt begins to sweat, then wipe with a dry cloth. Heat the
oil in a small saucepan and saute the garlic and all the vegetables, except the
tomatoes, until golden. Season to taste. Add the tomatoes and herbs, and saute
for a further 2–3 minutes.

GREEN BUNCHING ONION CASSEROLE

50 ml (2 fl oz) olive oil
4 small bunches small green bunching onions,
    peeled and with green left on
4 medium tomatoes, peeled, seeded and chopped

a large pinch of ground black pepper
25 g (1 oz) coriander seeds, ground and toasted
sea salt, to taste
bay leaf
½ bunch fresh coriander leaves

For the casserole, heat the oil in an enamelled cast-iron casserole and colour the
onions slightly. Add the rest of the ingredients, except the coriander, and cook,
covered, in an oven preheated to 200°C (400°F) for about 30 minutes. Mix in
the fresh coriander leaves and serve.

CUCUMBER SALAD

4 small Lebanese or telegraph cucumbers
2 medium red onions, peeled and sliced
½ bunch mint leaves
½ bunch fresh coriander leaves

150 ml (5 fl oz) fish sauce (Nom Pla)
75 ml (3 fl oz) rice vinegar
400 ml (14 fl oz) water
100 g (4 oz) sugar
3 small fresh red chillies, seeded and chopped

Wash and slice the cucumbers, with the skin on. Add the onions, mint and coriander
leaves, and mix together. Mix the fish sauce, vinegar, water and sugar together
to your taste, then add enough chilli to suit yourself. Pour over the other ingredients
and toss well, then let stand for a few hours before serving.

STINGAREE WINGS WITH PLUM TOMATOES IN BALSAMIC VINEGAR

S tingaree, the less common name for stingray, makes it seem less aggressive and much more edible.

It is Australia and New Zealand's largest ray and can grow up to a couple of metres long. However, the smallest and youngest wings are best for this recipe.

Larousse gives some useful hints about judging the freshness of this fish. The fresher it is, the more ammonia-like is its smell—it ought to be washed a few times before cooking to get rid of this as its coating will go on regenerating for 10 hours or so after death. Rub it with a cloth and see if the coating reappears.

The wings can also be barbecued and served with a dressing of butter mixed with chilli, pepper and lime, or more simply with olive oil and lemon and a fresh green salad.

SERVES 4–6

THE TOMATOES

250 g (9 oz) baby plum tomatoes (cherry tomatoes are a good substitute)
200 g (7 oz) yellow pear tomatoes
1 teaspoon sea salt
ground black pepper, to taste

4 tablespoons freshly chopped herbs, such as parsley, basil, mint or oregano
200 ml (7 fl oz) extra virgin olive oil
75 ml (3 fl oz) balsamic vinegar
1 small bunch red basil leaves

First prepare the tomatoes. Make a cross in the end of each tomato, then quickly blanch in boiling water. Refresh them in iced water and peel the skins.

Season the peeled tomatoes in a bowl with sea salt and black pepper, then toss with the chopped herbs. Sprinkle liberally with olive oil and vinegar, and set aside to improve.

THE STINGAREE

2 x 500 g (18 oz) stingaree/stingray wings, filleted
100 g (4 oz) unsalted butter

200 g (7 oz) plain flour, seasoned with salt and pepper
75g (3 oz) unsalted butter
4 tablespoons balsamic vinegar

Cut the stingaree fillets into strips of the desired portion size. Heat a heavy-based pan and add half the 100 g (4 oz) unsalted butter. The serving side of the wing is the piece that was against the bone, so lightly coat this side of the flesh with seasoned flour.

When the butter begins to foam, saute the wing pieces until browned. Turn the fish. Try to keep the butter foaming in the French method known as *meuniere* through the whole of the cooking, adding a knob of the butter from time to time to maintain the foam.

When the fish is cooked through remove it from the pan and keep warm. Discard the remaining butter. Reheat the same pan without cleaning it and add the 75 g (3 oz) butter. Cook this until it begins to brown, then deglaze with the balsamic vinegar to make a sauce.

To serve, arrange the fish pieces on plates and spoon the sauce on top. Add a couple of generous spoonfuls of the prepared tomatoes and tear a few red basil leaves over the top.

BALMAIN BUGS' TAILS, ROAST SQUASH AND CURRY DRESSING

These little antediluvian looking crustaceans used to be caught around Balmain in Sydney by local fishermen for their own consumption. They can now be bought fresh or pre-cooked. Since there is no way of knowing just how fresh the pre-cooked ones are, it is best to buy them raw and, if possible, alive.

Serve them out of their shells as they are easier to eat that way. To prepare, once the bugs have been cooked, pull the tails off and reserve the heads for bisque or stock. Cut down the inside of the tail shells with scissors and peel the shell off.

SERVES 4–6

THE CURRY BUTTER
6 French shallots, chopped
2 teaspoons Indonesian style curry powder
1 teaspoon olive oil

1 tablespoon white wine vinegar
1 tablespoon Choko and Pineapple Chutney
  (see page 167)
200 g (7 oz) unsalted butter, at room
  temperature

Lightly saute the shallots and curry powder in the oil, then add the vinegar and chutney, and cook slowly until most of the liquid has evaporated. Combine all the ingredients with the butter and roll into a long sausage on a sheet of foil moistened with a few drops of cold water. Reserve in the refrigerator until needed, or freeze if you have a longer plan for it.

THE SQUASH
500 g (18 oz) small variegated squash, topped
  and tailed

sea salt and pepper, to taste
75 ml (3 fl oz) olive oil

Season the squash with salt and pepper, heat the oil in a roasting pan and quickly colour each side. Add the reserved curry butter, chopped, and roast in an oven preheated to 200°C (400°F) until the squash are still quite crunchy when pierced with a knife.

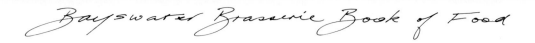

THE CURRY DRESSING

2 egg yolks

1 tablespoon white vinegar

½ teaspoon salt

freshly ground black pepper

} at room temperature

75 g (3 oz) Choko and Pineapple Chutney (see page 167)

1 tablespoon Indonesian style yellow curry powder, toasted

150 ml (5 fl oz) olive oil

To make the mayonnaise, mix the eggs, vinegar and seasoning in the food processor. Incorporate the chutney and curry powder, then add the oil in a thin stream. Reserve.

THE BUGS

2.3 kg (5 lb) Balmain bugs

½ bunch parsley stalks

juice of 4 lemons

Thoroughly wash and scrub the bugs, removing any eggs, then cook in boiling salted water with the parsley stalks and lemon juice. Bring it back to the boil. Drain the bugs and separate the tails, discarding the rest.

To serve, toss the tails in the curry mayonnaise and arrange on top of the squash.

CRYSTAL BOILED CHICKEN, CASHEW NUTS AND WATERCRESS

This is a very refreshing combination. The chicken is boiled with the flavours of sesame seed oil and orange, and served on a salad with crunchy cashews dressed with some of the chicken soup.

The left over, crystal clear, cooking liquid can be used as a delicious soup, served either hot or cold.

SERVES 4–6

THE CRYSTAL BOILED CHICKEN

2 x no.12 (1.2 kg or 2¾ lb each) cornfed or open range chickens

1.5 L (2½ pts) water

250 ml (9 fl oz) thin soy sauce

600 ml (20 fl oz) pale sweet sherry

12 whole star anise

zest of ½ an orange

Choose a saucepan that will hold the chickens without too much extra room around them. Cover with the rest of the ingredients and bring to the boil. Simmer slowly for 2 minutes. Take off the heat, cover and cool in the liquid to room temperature. Remove all fat.

Remove the chickens from the stock and shred the flesh, discarding the bones and skin. Strain the stock and use some of it over the salad, chilling the rest for future use.

82

THE SALAD

1 bunch shallots or spring onions

250 g (9 oz) cashew nuts

50 ml (2 fl oz) grape seed oil

1 bunch watercress, picked and washed

2 bunches kangkong, picked and washed

3 blood oranges or ruby grapefruits, peeled
  and segmented

4 small tomatoes, peeled, quartered and seeded

Peel, split and cut the shallots into 2.5 cm (1 in) lengths. Roast the cashews with a little grape seed oil in an oven preheated to 180°C (350°F), until they are golden brown.

THE DRESSING

30 ml (1 fl oz) rice vinegar

juice of ½ a lemon

1 teaspoon sesame seed oil

75 ml (3 fl oz) grape seed oil

sea salt and pepper, to taste

Make a dressing with the vinegar, lemon juice and oils and season with salt and pepper.

Not much dressing is needed for the salad, since it will also be moistened with the chicken liquid. Mix all the salad ingredients carefully together and toss with the dressing.

To serve, arrange the shredded chicken on top of the salad and sprinkle with the cashews. Pour over some of the reserved crystal chicken liquid.

CHICKEN CONGEE WITH DRIED PRAWNS AND
FRIED GINGER DUMPLINGS

Rice porridge or congee is served as a breakfast dish in Asia. Traditionally the Asian dish was made with the broken grains of rice left over from the mills. It makes a wonderful grain base, which can easily take up the whole range of hot or spicy flavours and can be served with a variety of seafoods, vegetables and meats.

This version, served in a large bowl with dumplings and a selection of garnishes, is a dish designed for a wintry lunch.

SERVES 6–8

THE CONGEE

1 x 1.2 kg (2¾ lb) boiling chicken

3 L (5 pts) Chicken Stock (page 23)

75 g (3 oz) long grain rice

75 g (3 oz) short grain rice

50 ml (2 fl oz) vegetable oil

1 x 6 cm (2½ in) piece ginger, grated

100 g (4 oz) dried prawns, soaked in water
  for 1 hour and washed

To cook the chicken, cover it with cold water, bring to the boil, and drain. Cover with the chicken stock and return it to the boil, skim, then simmer for another 10 minutes. Remove from the heat and leave the chicken in the stock for another 30 minutes to cook through. Drain the stock and remove the flesh from the chicken. Discard the skin and chop the meat.

Wash the rice several times and dry it thoroughly. Heat the vegetable oil in a heavy-based pan, add the rice and ginger, and saute. Stir the rice until it begins to crackle. Reheat the reserved stock and pour it over the rice, then bring it to the boil, stirring constantly to prevent it sticking. Simmer first over medium heat, then reduce to low, stirring from time to time, and being careful to lift the mixture up and away from the bottom of the pan. Cooking takes about 1½ hours and during this time the rice will slowly burst and become gluey. Stir through the chicken meat and the softened prawns.

THE FRIED GINGER DUMPLINGS
225 ml (8 fl oz) water
120 g (4 oz) butter, chopped
1 x 6 cm (2½ in) root of ginger, peeled and grated
grated zest of 2 lemons
225 g (8 oz) plain flour
pinch of salt mixed with pinch of sugar
5 eggs
grape seed or vegetable oil for deep frying

To make the dumplings, bring the water to the boil in a saucepan with the butter, ginger and lemon zest until the butter just melts. Put the flour, with the salt and sugar mixture, in the middle of a large sheet of kitchen paper and pour in a steady stream into the simmering mixture. Stir until it comes away from the sides of the pan, then cook for another 2 minutes. Remove from the heat and let it cool slightly.

Mix in the eggs one at a time, then scrape the mixture into a piping bag with a wide piping tube, or with no tube at all.

Heat some oil in a deep frying pan and squeeze in 10–12 cm (4–5 in) lengths of dumpling mixture. Fry until golden brown on each side. These are either chopped or served whole scattered on top of the congee.

THE GARNISHES
175 g (6 oz) peanuts, fried in a pan with a little oil
½ a shredded iceberg lettuce
½ bunch chopped spring onions
½ bunch coarsely chopped coriander leaves

To serve, ladle the congee into large bowls and sprinkle the dumplings and prepared garnishes on top. Serve with a heavy soy sauce and, if your taste is for hot things, a chilli sauce on the side.

STEAMED CHOY SUM WITH SHREDDED DUCK AND EGG

The idea for this dish came from the Chinese restaurant dishes of bright green, crisp vegetables floating in a gently aromatic soup or stock. Choy sum is a Cantonese variety of cabbage which tastes like a cross between the common cabbage and collard greens. Madhur Jaffrey quite rightly observes that once you have discovered this vegetable you are unlikely to give it up.

The duck has been treated in the same way as Peking Duck and we owe the culinary use of the hair drier to Marcella Hazan.

SERVES 4–6

THE DUCK

1 kg (2 lb 3 oz) plump duck

50 ml (2 fl oz) honey

100 ml (3½ fl oz) thick soy sauce

50 ml (2 fl oz) medium dry sherry

100 ml (3½ fl oz) water

Tie a string around the bird's legs and plunge it into briskly boiling water for 1–2 minutes. Remove from water then hang it up to drain and dry. This opens the skin pores and keeps them open during cooking. One good way to achieve this is to dry the duck off with a hair drier on the hot setting for 10 minutes. The open pores absorb the flavours of the marinade better and ensure that the duck flesh stays moist without being fatty or greasy.

Make a marinade with the honey, soy sauce, sherry and water, and paint the duck with 3–4 coats, letting it dry in between. You can use the drier for this too, but on a lower heat or at a reasonable distance to avoid exhausting the skin. Leave the painted duck overnight in a cool place.

Roast the duck on a cake rack in an oven preheated to 170°C (325°F) for 1½ hours or until the skin is brown and crisp. If you do not have a fan oven, turn the duck around a few times during roasting. After roasting, let the duck rest for a while in a warm place until cool enough to handle. Skin it with a sharp knife and set the skin aside, then take the meat off the bones and shred.

THE CHOY SUM SOUP

6 small pieces choy sum

6 pieces star anise

4 eggs, beaten

1 L (1²/₃ pts) Duck Stock (see page 23), reduced to 500 ml (18 fl oz)

3 tablespoons toasted pecan nuts

Blanch the choy sum in boiling salted water flavoured with the star anise. Dry fry the eggs in a wok until they are set and slightly brown.

To serve, place the choy sum in a deep dish and pour the hot stock over. Add the shredded duck meat, cooked egg and toasted pecan nuts, and top the soup with pieces of crisp duck skin.

SAUTEED CHICKEN BREAST, COUSCOUS AND CHILLI JAM

C ouscous is a national dish of North Africa. In Morocco, Tunisia and Algeria it is traditionally served steamed with a broth or stew made from a variety of vegetables, seafood, chicken, game or lamb and sometimes with chickpeas and raisins. It is also served with a hot chilli sauce called *harissa*.

In this dish I have substituted the Asian chilli jam called *mae pronom* for the harissa. You can make your own, but chilli out of control in the domestic kitchen is not much fun, so do the sensible thing and buy it ready made from an Asian food store.

Couscous is a cereal mostly produced from semolina, the hard part of the wheat grain. It is sometimes made from barley, and in Tunisia from green wheat, and is an extremely useful and versatile carbohydrate component of the meal. Like rice and noodles, it easily takes up and sustains the flavours of the rest of the dish. The couscous I use is precooked and packed dry.

SERVES 4

THE CHICKEN

8 small chicken breasts

100 g (4 oz) plain flour

150 ml (5 fl oz) olive oil

salt and pepper, to taste

2 red capsicums, grilled, peeled and cut in strips

Lightly dust each chicken breast with the flour and saute in the oil until the skin side is a golden brown. Turn the breasts over, season with salt and pepper and cook for a further 3–4 minutes in an oven preheated to 180°C (350°F).

THE COUSCOUS

350 ml (12 fl oz) water

250 g (9 oz) couscous

400 ml (14 fl oz) Chicken Consomme (see page 23)

3 tablepoons clarified butter

2 medium leeks, shredded

salt and pepper, to taste

4 teaspoons chilli jam (mae pronom)

¼ bunch chopped parsley

Boil the water, pour it over the couscous and let it swell. Heat the chicken consomme and keep it warm. Heat the clarified butter in a large heavy-based pan and saute the leeks until they soften. Add the couscous and cook at a reasonable heat for 2–3 minutes until it is slightly coloured. Check the seasoning, and correct if necessary.

Serve a pile of couscous in the middle of each plate, place two chicken breasts on the pile and garnish with the strips of red capsicum and a teaspoon of the chilli jam. Pour a liberal amount of the consomme, which has had the parsley added to it, around the edge of each dish.

POACHED VEAL TONGUE WITH MUSTARD AND CHERVIL DRESSING

Veal tongues are an excellent lunch meat that works well in combination with Crystal Boiled Chicken (see page 82) or slices of filetto, the salt-cured, dried loin of pork, and a robust salad. It can also be served for lunch with the Goat Cheese Tart (see page 35) which we have included among the breakfast dishes or the Roast Potato Tart (see page 174).

SERVES 4–6

THE TONGUE
4 x 125 g (4 oz) veal tongues
½ recipe of Brine (see page 42)

salt and pepper, to taste
1 large onion, sliced
2 medium leeks, white ends sliced

Blanch the tongues quickly in fresh boiling water, then skin and remove any cartilage. Prick them with a trussing needle, put them under a weight, then soak in the brine overnight. Simmer the tongues in water seasoned with the salt, pepper, onion and leeks for a couple of hours, or until tender. Leave the tongues in the stock just until warm.

THE MUSTARD DRESSING
50 ml (2 fl oz) white wine vinegar
1 tablespoon Dijon mustard
100 ml (3½ fl oz) olive oil

100 ml (3½ fl oz) grape seed oil
2 bunches chervil, chopped
½ bunch chives, chopped
salt and pepper, to taste

Mix together the vinegar and mustard, and whisk the oils into them. Add the chervil and chives to the vinaigrette. Slice the warm tongue, then season and toss with the vinaigrette.

BARBECUED RARE BEEF, BEETROOTS AND PEPPER MAYONNAISE

This is an ideal outdoor lunch which you can prepare in advance. The rare beef and beetroots are an attractive combination with the dark green watercress leaves of the garnish. You will need to have some good strong veal stock on hand to make the dish, preferably flavoured with bay leaves.

First heat the barbecue. Getting this right has a lot to do with the success or failure of any barbecued dish, which might seem to be stating the obvious, but still needs to be said. Never use an accelerant on your barbecue coals from the point of view of safety and because accelerant flavours can linger on and taint the cooking. Start your fire with good kindling and have a little patience in building up a good red-hot base of coals to cook on. Keep the heat trapped inside the pile of coals until you spread them for the cooking.

SERVES 4

THE BEETROOTS

16 baby beetroots, scrubbed

1 L (1²/₃ pts) water

250 ml (9 fl oz) white vinegar

2 tablespoons brown sugar

2 teaspoons salt

1 teaspoon whole peppercorns

1 bunch watercress

Put all the ingredients, except the watercress, into a pan covered with water. Bring them to the boil and simmer until the beets are tender on the outside but still reasonably firm and crisp at the centre. Remove and let them cool enough to handle. Peel the beets under running water, wearing rubber gloves. Be careful to retain about 8 cm (3 in) of the tops for aesthetic reasons.

While the beets are cooking, wash and pick the watercress, then leave submerged in a bowl of water in the refrigerator.

THE BEEF

700 g (1½ lb) beef fillet, cleaned

1 L (1²/₃ pints) Veal Stock (see page 22), reduced to half

2–3 fresh bay leaves

Thoroughly sear the beef on the barbecue until it is black on the outside and rare inside. Heat the stock with the bay leaves. Put the beef in a pan, cover with the hot stock and let it sit, off the heat.

THE MAYONNAISE

2 egg yolks

1 tablespoon white wine vinegar

3 tablespoons freshly ground black pepper

1 teaspoon sugar

½ teaspoon salt

2 teaspoons Dijon mustard

150 ml (5 fl oz) olive oil

You can make the mayonnaise in a food processor or whisk it in a bowl. Make sure the ingredients are at room temperature. Whisk all the ingredients, except the oil, together. Whisk, or if you are using a food processor, pour the oil in a thin thread onto the other ingredients until they are creamy and thick.

To serve, take the beef out of the stock, reserving 50 ml (2 fl oz), and cut it into slices approximately 1 cm (½ in) thick; it should be rare enough inside to please a vampire and crisp black around the edges. Arrange three slices on each plate with a pile of the beetroots, which have been tossed with the drained cress. Bring some of the reserved stock to the boil and thin the mayonnaise with it. Drizzle a ladle of this around each plate.

STUFFED PORK TROTTERS WITH SAUTEED POTATOES
AND LEMON

An excellent example of the complexity of the kind of charcuterie dishes the Brasserie serves is the Bayswater's Stuffed Pork Trotters. It takes some time and some skill, but it is a marvellous transformation of the least important of the pig's edible bits into something quite grand.

SERVES 6

THE BRINE AND TROTTERS

2 L (3½ pt) brine (see page 42)

6 medium trotters, cleaned

Make the brine and wrap each pair of trotters in muslin with the toes of each pointing in opposite directions like a mad ballet dancer. Bind them with butcher's twine, cover with the brine and soak overnight.

THE COURT BOUILLON

4 medium carrots

2 medium onions, stuck with 2 cloves

4 sticks celery

1 clove garlic

500 ml (18 fl oz) white wine

1 teaspoon black peppercorns

2 bay leaves, preferably fresh

1 tablespoon salt

*2 L (3½ pts) Veal Stock (see page 22) or
  water*

Combine all the ingredients, then add the muslin-wrapped trotters. Bring this to the boil and simmer, skimming frequently, for 3 hours or until a paring knife can be easily pushed through the meat. The trotters should not be cooked to the point of disintegration. Let the trotters cool in the bouillon.

THE STUFFING

12 sheets of pigs caul 20 cm (8 in) square

½ recipe Pork Sausage Filling (see page 26)

Soak the caul in cold water for a couple of hours.

Remove the trotters from the bouillon, then strain and reserve the liquid. Unwrap the trotters and split the skin on the underside of each. Carefully remove all the bones, leaving only the tiny bone in each toe. Try not to split the skin on the top of the trotter, however if you do, don't panic, as the finished stuffed trotter is going to be wrapped in the caul.

Divide the pork sausage filling into six and roll each portion into a sausage shape about the length of a trotter. Fill each deboned trotter with the sausage filling, then try to press it back to the original trotter shape. Wrap each trotter with 2 sheets of pigs caul and tie, not too tightly, with butcher's twine. Cover the trotters with the reserved bouillon, bring to the boil and simmer for 1 hour. Let them cool in the liquid. These can be stored in the refrigerator or prepared for serving immediately.

THE FINAL STAGE
250 g (9 oz) melted butter
200 g (7 oz) soft breadcrumbs
100 ml (3½ fl oz) grape seed oil
4 tablespoons unsalted butter
24 small potatoes, cooked in their skins and
  sliced

salt and pepper, to taste
juice of 1 lemon
½ bunch chopped parsley
500 mls (18 fl oz) Veal Stock (page 22),
  reduced to 100 ml (3½ fl oz)

Remove the string from each trotter, then roll each in the melted butter and then in the crumbs. Heat the oil in a heavy-based pan, put the trotters in topside up, tilt the pan and baste them with some of the hot oil. Grill them for 10–12 minutes under a hot grill until they are well browned and heated through.

While the trotters are grilling, heat the unsalted butter in a black steel pan. When it begins to foam, toss in the potatoes and cook until they are golden and crisp. Transfer to a dish, season and keep warm in the oven.

To the remaining butter in the pan, add the lemon juice and parsley. Heat the veal stock. Spoon the stock onto one half of each serving plate, then add lemon butter to the other half, being careful not to allow them to mix so as to retain the separate flavours of each. Arrange the trotters and potatoes around or on the sauces, in some suitably elegant way, and serve.

Dinner

Of all feasts, none has proved more moveable than dinner. In Europe at least. It began as the first meal of the day, shifted to the middle, then the early afternoon, and in our times has finally arrived at the evening. Some people, of course, still consume it in the middle of the day and reserve the evening for tea or supper, and a generation ago in Australia and New Zealand, dinners were formal affairs eaten in hotel dining rooms or at home at midday on a Sunday.

One thing that we share with our more recent ancestors is the notion that dinner, whenever it might be offered or eaten, can be mainly an occasion to entertain. As Sir W. S. Gilbert put it, "It isn't so much what's on the table that matters as what's on the chairs." Lin Yutang was even more certain that "the object of a dinner is not to eat and drink, but to join in merry making and make a lot of noise."

Dinners in days past were formidable affairs and it is little wonder, with some of them stretching to ten or fifteen courses, that diners lost sight of what was on the table. Still, as somebody put it, the past is a place where things are done differently, and while we still favour the merry making and reasonable joyful noise, what we eat is the proof not only of the pudding but of the whole meal.

Essentially the whole basis of the brasserie style is simplicity done to perfection— not vast symphonies of courses, but trios and quartets. The dishes must deserve the company, but they ought not to dominate. It might once have been true, as Dr Johnson put it, that "a man seldom thinks with more earnestness of anything than he does of his dinner", but earnestness is not, we hope, a characteristic of the brasserie style.

The best meals are those which are recalled as a total event, not as a series of gourmet feats. That suits our lifestyles best and while some of the dishes here do require complex processes, the majority of them can be finished quickly and with style, allowing the last part of the preparation either to be a part of the entertainment or not too much of an intrusion as to keep the cooks away from their guests for too long.

It is fair to say that the mark of a good brasserie is a connection between the diners and the kitchen—a relationship of sights, sounds and cooking smells that stimulates the appetite, the thirst and the conversation.

FIELD MUSHROOM PUREE

The best mushrooms for this dish are those you find in country paddocks on humid autumn days. The cultivated field mushrooms will do, but apart from the romance of gathering them, there is nothing quite like the strong, musty flavour of the wild variety. In this thick black soup, the mushrooms do all the thickening on their own account.

THE PUREE
1.2 kg (2¼ lb) field mushrooms
150 g (5 oz) unsalted butter
65 g (2½ oz) purple eshallots, peeled and chopped
salt and pepper, to taste

700 ml (1¼ pts) Veal Stock (see page 22)
4 tablespoons white wine vinegar
1 bunch tarragon leaves
½ bunch chives, chopped
200 ml (7 fl oz) double cream

Clean the mushrooms with a dry cloth, trim and scrape the stalks, then roughly chop them. Heat the butter in a saucepan and when it begins to foam, add the mushrooms and eshallots. Season and saute them for about 5 minutes.

In another pan, bring the stock to the boil and pour it over the sauteed mushrooms and eshallots. Add the vinegar, season with salt and pepper and return it to the boil. Simmer for another 15 minutes. Add the tarragon leaves, bring it back to the boil and simmer for a further 5 minutes. Puree in a blender, then pass through the medium grill of a food mill. Reheat the puree in a clean pan.

Serve in bowls with a sprinkle of chopped chives and a dollop of double cream.

RUGGED MUSSEL CHOWDER

There is more than a touch of salty romance about a chowder although, surprisingly, the dish can be made with chicken or corn and not come within sight of the sea. The name most probably derives from the French fish soup of the Vendee and Saintonge coasts which is called *chaudree*, although some sources have it coming from *chaudiere* or boiler. Whatever its origins chowder is a genuine meal in a plate.

One of the most famous chowders is from New England, USA, and is made with clams. There is a derivative of this with tomato sauce called Manhattan Chowder. Both these are creamy textured but the dish we offer is more like the traditional chowders, with the diced potatoes staying recognisable to the end.

Serve this with croutons floating in it or with slices of crunchy bread, even partly toasted if you like.

SERVES 4–6

THE MUSSELS

3 kg (6 lb 10 oz) mussels

300 ml (11 fl oz) white wine

300 ml (11 fl oz) Fish Stock (see page 23)

½ bunch parsley stalks (chop the leaves and
save for the soup)

1 teaspoon cracked pepper

Clean the mussels and steam them in the wine and fish stock with the parsley
and cracked pepper. Remove them as they open, being careful to pour any juice
back into the pan, and discard any shells that stay shut. Reserve the liquid in
the covered pan. Remove the mussels from their shells and roughly chop them.

THE SOUP

6 strips of wakame seaweed, soaked in cold
water for 10 minutes

100 g (4 oz) butter

100 g lean bacon, chopped

1 large potato, chopped

4 red capsicums, cleaned and chopped

1 small head of celeriac, chopped

2 medium onions, chopped

2 medium leeks, chopped

2 bay leaves

salt and pepper, to taste

400 ml (14 fl oz) milk

½ bunch parsley, chopped

Drain the seaweed, then slice and cut into 2 cm (¾ in) pieces. Heat the butter
in a large heavy-based pan and saute the bacon for about 5 minutes. Add the
vegetables and saute for another 5 minutes. Pour in 1L (1⅔ pts) cooking liquid
from the mussels, add the bay leaves and seaweed, and lightly season.

Simmer for another 20 minutes or so until the potato is cooked. Add the
chopped mussels and the milk, and bring back to the boil. Serve in a large bowl
with the chopped parsley and croutons or crunchy bread.

DUCK LIVER MOUSSE ON BRIOCHE TOAST WITH ROCKET SALAD

The Brioche loaf (see page 32) is a useful base for entrees of this kind.
For this dish you will need one 2 cm (¾ in) thick slice for each serve.
Of course if you have a foie gras in your pantry the rest of this recipe
is entirely superfluous. For those who do not, half a recipe of brioche is sufficient
to serve with the mousse.

SERVES 4–6

THE DUCK LIVER MOUSSE

400 g (14 oz) duck's livers

8 tablespoons brandy

125 g (4 oz) butter

salt and pepper, to taste

50 ml (2 fl oz) double cream

Clean the livers of all sinew, dry them, then marinate in half the brandy for 2 hours.

Heat the butter in a large heavy-based pan until foaming. Season the livers with salt and pepper. Throw the livers in the pan and turn them almost immediately, so they cook quickly and are very pink inside. Remove when they are beginning to seal on all sides, and let them cool.

Deglaze the pan juices with the remaining brandy. Add the livers to the brandy, then pass through the medium grill of a food mill. (A food processor is not suitable to use in this instance as the livers will continue cooking in the processor and be overcooked.) Fold the double cream through the mix, pass it through the fine grill of a food mill again, check for seasoning and refrigerate.

THE ROCKET SALAD
4 bunches young rocket leaves, washed and dried
1 punnet of cherry tomatoes, halved
2 tablespoons olive oil
2 tablespoons sherry vinegar
salt and pepper, to taste

Toss the rocket leaves, tomatoes, oil and vinegar together and season.

Shortly before serving, slice the brioche diagonally, then spread liberally with the mousse. Heap the salad in the centre of each plate and tuck the still warm toast into either side.

COS LETTUCE SALAD WITH FILETTO

It is becoming fashionable to follow the tradition in some parts of Europe of serving a salad after the main course. For some main courses it is not a bad idea to follow with something equally as refreshing, but less flippant, than a cold pudding. It is certainly a far better choice between courses than the barbaric habit of destroying the wine with a sorbet.

If you intend to serve this after a main course as a refresher, skip the filetto. If you can't get filetto, prosciutto or Parma ham will do as well.

THE DRESSING
2 egg yolks, at room temperature
2 tablespoons white wine vinegar
1 teaspoon mustard
salt and pepper, to taste
275 ml (10 fl oz) olive oil

Mix the egg yolks, vinegar, mustard, salt and pepper together, then whisk in the oil in a thread.

5 eggs
8 anchovy fillets, washed and dried
a few drops chilli oil
1 tablespoon lemon juice

Boil the eggs, starting with cold water, until the whites are set and the yolks are still runny. If the eggs are at room temperature, this will take about 4 minutes from the start of boiling. Carefully peel and mash them in a bowl with the anchovy fillets, chilli oil and lemon juice. Just before serving, lightly whisk this mixture into the mayonnaise and check the seasoning.

THE SALAD
36 x 2 cm (¾ in) square croutons, cut from
  thin slices of foccacia bread
4 tablespoons melted butter
4 tablespoons grated Parmesan cheese
good pinch of freshly ground black pepper

pinch of cayenne pepper
100 g (4 oz) piece Parmesan cheese
cos lettuce, washed and dried
Italian parsley leaves
200 g (7 oz) filetto, thinly sliced

Dip the croutons in the melted butter and sprinkle with grated Parmesan, pepper and cayenne. Toast the croutons under a grill until golden. Slice the chunk of Parmesan into wedges.

Arrange the cos and parsley in a bowl and toss with the egg, anchovy and mayonnaise mixture. Serve the salad on plates with the croutons and filetto slices, and the Parmesan wedges tucked in.

VEAL SWEETBREADS AND GRILLED CAPSICUMS WITH ONION AND RAISIN RELISH

Sweetbreads are the thymus or pancreas glands of calves, lambs and, very rarely, pigs. Sweetbreads are easily digested, high in protein and low in fibre, and for these reasons gained a reputation as a suitable meal for invalids. They deserve better than that and are, in fact, an ideal vehicle for strong and spicy flavours.

SERVES 4–6
THE SWEETBREADS
700 g (1½ lb) veal sweetbreads
900 ml (1⅔ pts) Chicken Stock (see page 23)

juice of 1 lemon
2 red capsicums, grilled and peeled
2 yellow capsicums, grilled and peeled

Soak the sweetbreads overnight in cold salted water. Sharpen the chicken stock with the lemon juice and bring it to the boil. Add the sweetbreads, let the liquid come back to the boil, reduce the heat and simmer for 2 minutes. Let the sweetbreads cool in the stock, then remove them, cut off any membranes and slice.

THE RELISH
24 green onions, peeled and chopped
1 hot chilli, cleaned and seeded
2 bay leaves
2 cloves

2 tablespoons brown sugar
2 tablespoons red wine vinegar
200 ml (7 fl oz) Chicken Stock (see page 23)
3 tablespoons currants
pinch of salt and some finely ground black
      pepper

Put all the ingredients in a saucepan and simmer for about 30 minutes, or until the onions are cooked and the mixture has the consistency of a thin marmalade.

TO SERVE
butter
flour, seasoned with salt and pepper
juice of 1 lemon

2 tablespoons capers
virgin olive oil

Heat the butter in a heavy-based pan, dredge the sweetbreads in the flour and saute until they are golden brown on each side. Remove, drain and season with salt and pepper. Add the lemon juice to the butter remaining in the pan, remove from the heat and return the sweetbreads, tossing to coat them.

Arrange the capsicum slices on the plates, sprinkle with the capers and the olive oil, spoon a generous helping of relish over them and put the hot sweetbread slices on top.

BUCKWHEAT BLINIS WITH KRILL AND RADISH SPROUTS

Krill are tiny crustaceans that go about the ocean in vast swarms. Whales do very well on them and so do the Japanese who still, regrettably, like to eat the whales as well.

Waverley Root reports that in certain parts of the southern oceans, where the whales have been hunted almost to extinction, the unassailed krill boil about in such large numbers that the sea looks like some kind of seafood soup. Such are the cycles in these things, that some fishermen report that krill off the New Zealand coasts, where whales are now unmolested, are being hunted almost to extinction, so the seas there might soon be boiling with hungry whales!

Blinis are a Russian or Polish invention. They are a small pancake of buckwheat flour which, with a large amount of savoury garnish, is traditionally a base for caviar. For those of us for whom caviar is a very rare dish, they can also be served with smoked salmon, mussels, smoked fish, kippers or, as in this dish, with krill and salmon roe.

SERVES 4–6

THE BLINIS

15 g (½ oz) fresh yeast	2 eggs
1½ tablespoons tepid water	200 ml (7 fl oz) tepid milk
200 g (7 oz) buckwheat flour	200 ml (7 fl oz) clarified butter

Dissolve the yeast in the tepid water, add the buckwheat flour and eggs, and mix together. Gradually beat in the milk. Rest the mixture for 1½ hours to let the yeast grow, making quite a thick batter.

To cook the blinis, heat a crepe pan and add a tablespoon of the clarified butter. When this is "frying hot", drop in a 50 ml (2 fl oz) ladleful of batter. When the bubbles appear on the uncooked side and it looks rather like a raw crumpet, turn it over and brown the bottom. Continue until all the batter has been used. The blinis should be nicely brown and crisp on both sides. Keep them warm on a rack in the oven.

THE ROE, KRILL AND RADISHES

4–6 spring onions, cleaned	salt and pepper, to taste
1 punnet of radish sprouts	75 ml (3 fl oz) Creme Fraiche (see page 57)
300 g (11 oz) krill	50 g (2 oz) salmon roe
	1–2 lemons, cut in wedges

Split and chop the spring onions, then mix with the radish sprouts and krill. Season with salt and a good grinding of pepper.

Spread a tablespoon of the creme fraiche on each blini, pile the mixed ingredients on top, finish with a teaspoon of salmon roe, and serve with a lemon wedge on the side.

FRIED ARTICHOKES WITH TOMATO AND BASIL VINAIGRETTE

The globe artichoke is a very versatile thing. It can be stuffed, boiled, stewed into a risotto or, when they are small and young, eaten raw. This dish is a great spring combination; the cool and elegant tomatoes with the sizzling hot artichokes crusted with Parmesan cheese and blessed with a sweet-sharp basil sauce.

SERVES 4–6

THE BASIL VINAIGRETTE

150 ml (5 fl oz) virgin olive oil	salt and pepper, to taste
50 ml (2 fl oz) balsamic vinegar	½ bunch green and purple basil

Make this shortly before serving and chop the basil leaves at the very last minute. Whisk the oil slowly onto the vinegar, salt and pepper. Chop the basil and mix it thoroughly through the vinaigrette, making sure the leaves are quickly coated to preserve the colour and flavour.

THE TOMATOES

4–6 tomatoes, blanched and peeled

2 tablespoons olive oil

juice of 1 lime

sea salt and pepper, to taste

Cut each tomato into 8 pieces. Dress with the oil and juice, and season with salt and pepper. This can sit for a while at room temperature.

THE ARTICHOKES

12 young globe artichokes

1 lemon, halved

juice of 1 lemon

100 g (4 oz) Parmesan cheese

200 g (7 oz) breadcrumbs

4 eggs

2 L (3½ pts) grape seed oil

Remove the dark green outer leaves from the artichokes and peel the bases and stems. Rub the half lemon over the peeled parts, sit them in a pan of cold water and add the lemon juice. Bring the artichokes to the boil in the acidulated water and let them cook for about 15 minutes, or until they are tender to the point of a knife. Set them aside to cool in the liquid.

Grate the cheese into the breadcrumbs. Beat the eggs together. Pull the leaves off the artichokes, keeping the tender ones, and dip them, with the bases and stems, into the egg. Crumb them in the cheese and bread mixture and deep fry at 185°C (350°F) until crisp and brown.

Spoon the basil vinaigrette onto the plates. Cover with the tomatoes and serve the fried artichokes on top.

RAW BEEF, ONIONS AND PARMESAN WITH OLIVE OIL AND BLACK PEPPER

Any dish of dressed raw beef with pretensions to Italian origins is widely and wrongly known as *carpaccio*. The authentic version dresses the meat with a mustard, brandy and tabasco mayonnaise and was devised in a Venetian bar in 1961. It was named for the sixteenth century Venetian painter Vittorio Carpaccio, whose reds reminded the inventive chef of raw beef.

In whatever way the dish is served or named, it is essential not to dress it until immediately before serving, otherwise the attractive red of the beef will begin to look muddy.

SERVES 4–6

THE BEEF

*300 g (11 oz) sirloin of beef, trimmed of fat
and sinew and well chilled*

THE ONION DRESSING

6 medium Spanish onions, peeled and finely diced

juice of 2 lemons

125 ml (4 fl oz) extra virgin olive oil

500 ml (18 fl oz) olive oil

½ teaspoon sea salt

2 teaspoons ground black pepper

2 tablespoons grated Parmesan cheese

Combine all dressing ingredients, except the black pepper and the Parmesan cheese, and leave for at least 2 hours in the refrigerator.

Cut the meat into paper thin slices. Cover the surface of each plate with the slices of meat. Spread each plate with about 2 tablespoons of the onion dressing. Grind black pepper over the meat and onion mixture. Serve immediately.

SLICED VEAL TONGUE WITH A BUCKWHEAT NOODLE SALAD

This dish of cold buckwheat noodles, sharply dressed in a crunchy salad, also makes a fine summer lunch. The Japanese are fond of cold buckwheat or green tea noodles served on ice beside a sweet soup.

Because buckwheat doesn't have any gluten we have added some plain flour and gluten flour to give the noodles elasticity. Without it they would be completely brittle, like an illiterate alphabet pasta entirely confined to the letter "I".

SERVES 4–6

THE NOODLES

150 g (5 oz) buckwheat flour

50 g (2 oz) plain flour

2 tablespoons gluten flour

pinch of salt

pinch of pepper

2 eggs

fine semolina, for dusting

a few drops cold water, for extra moisture

Make fine noodles, as on page 163.

HORSERADISH VINAIGRETTE

2 tablespoons grated horseradish

50 ml (2 fl oz) white wine vinegar

salt and pepper, to taste

150 ml (5 fl oz) grape seed oil

Whisk the horseradish with the vinegar, salt and pepper, then add the oil in a steady stream.

THE SALAD

200 g (7 oz) snow peas

200 g (7 oz) broccoli

1 bulb of witloof, washed and broken into
   leaves

1 x 1 kg (2 lb 3 oz) Crystal Boiled Chicken
   (see page 82)

4 tablespoons olive oil

salt and pepper, to taste

1 pickled Veal Tongue (see page 87)

sea salt and freshly ground black pepper

Blanch the snow peas and broccoli and refresh in ice water. They will take slightly different times so cook them separately. Toss the snow peas, broccoli and witloof with the horseradish vinaigrette. Shred the flesh from the chicken.

Cook the noodles in boiling salted water until al dente and refresh them in iced water. Drain and coat them with the olive oil, then season with salt and pepper.

To serve, divide the noodles evenly onto the plates, cover with the salad and top that with the chicken. Fan thin slices of the veal tongue on the side and season the whole with sea salt and black pepper.

GARLIC CHIVE RISOTTO AND SEARED SCALLOPS

The first rule about this dish is that if you do not have the right rice, forget it! There are something like 2500 varieties of rice and, according to the cooks of Lombardy, Piedmont and Venice who perfected this dish, only one of them is right—Arborio—a large, long grained rice with great clinging qualities.

Rice varieties, apart from variation in colour, which is immense, are characterised by the amount of waxy starch molecules, *amylopectin*, they contain. Of the rice we are familiar with, the range is between Indian rice, which has the least, and is long grained, dry and flaky when cooked, and Japanese, which is small, round, moist and gluggy.

Arborio has just the right amount of *amylopectin* for risotto. It will cook to a firm al dente, while still having enough cling to bind the dish and keep it moist. That doyenne of Italian cooking teachers, Marcella Hazan, names two other Italian rice varieties, Vialone Nano and Carnaroli, which, as well as Arborio, are the best for risotto, and three others, Roma, Razza 77 and Maratelli, which will do.

As well as the right rice you will also need the right pan. It must be heavy-based to hold and pass on a consistent heat without letting the rice and broth mixture stew. Enamelled cast iron is ideal.

The dish is also labour intensive and requires constant attention during cooking. For those who like to cook and entertain, it's an ideal vehicle, and as it is one that must go almost immediately from stove to bowl, it needs a reasonable amount of thoughtful organisation.

SERVES 4–6

THE CHIVE PUREE

2 bunches garlic chives

2 tablespoons thick soy sauce

2 tablespoons thin soy sauce

Chop the chives roughly and blanch in boiling water for 2–3 minutes until they are soft but not losing any colour. Refresh in iced water and drain well. Put the chives, together with the soy sauces, in a food processor and puree until very smooth. This should be dark green in colour and thick enough to stand a spoon in. Set aside.

THE RISOTTO

1.1 L (2 pts) Fish Stock (see page 23), spiked
    with a pinch of saffron threads

75 g (3 oz) butter

1 small onion

375 g (13 oz) Arborio rice

salt and pepper, to taste

Bring the stock to the boil and keep it on a low simmer.

Melt the butter in a heavy-based pan and gently saute the onion until it is translucent. Add the rice and stir until each grain is covered with the butter. Pour in a third of the stock, and stir until the rice has absorbed it. Keep adding the stock bit by bit until the rice is cooked al dente. This will take about 20 minutes and requires concentration to ensure that the rice does not stew or overcook. Right up until the last minute the grains will be slightly chalky to the bite, and when this changes to firm but moist, the risotto is done.

At the end of cooking, stir through the chive puree. Check the seasoning and serve it straight onto plates.

THE SCALLOPS

2 tablespoons grape seed oil

500 g (18 oz) large dry scallops
    with roe, or 5 per serving

sea salt and pepper, to taste

2 tablespoons melted butter

juice of 1 lime

Heat a flat or ribbed black steel grill until very hot. Brush with a very small amount of oil. Season the scallops and sear them for 20 seconds on each side. Heat the melted butter in a pan and add the lime juice. Divide the scallops into 4–6 portions and arrange them over the rice. Glaze the scallops with the lime butter.

POACHED TUNA, POTATOES, FRESH BEANS AND ONION PICKLES

This is a reasonably simple dish and it can be made just as well with ocean trout or Atlantic salmon. The fish needs to be poached to perfection—not completely cooked through, and still moist—for the dish to succeed. The onion pickle is easy to make but needs to be made well in advance. It is a useful garnish to have in store.

SERVES 4–6

THE ONION PICKLE

3 red Spanish onions, peeled
4 tablespoons sea salt
375 ml (13 fl oz) white wine vinegar

175 g (6 oz) caster sugar
1 hot chilli, split and seeded
2 bay leaves
1 tablespoon grated horseradish

Slice and salt the onions, and set to one side. Bring all the remaining ingredients to the boil. Drain and remove the excess salt from the onions, then pour the hot pickling liquid over them. Cool for at least 3 hours and store in an airtight jar.

THE FISH

600 g (1¼ lb) tuna back steak in one piece
3 medium-sized red Spanish onions
2 L (3½ pts) Fish Stock (see page 23)
½ bunch parsley
½ bunch basil

1 bay leaf
1 teaspoon peppercorns
1 clove garlic
1 hot chilli, seeded
juice of 2 oranges
sea salt, to taste

Reserve the fish and make a court bouillon from the other ingredients. Let this simmer for 10 minutes, then add the fish and bring it back to the boil. Let it simmer for 1 minute more. Remove from the heat and cool until warm.

THE SALAD

4–6 medium desiree or Tasmanian pink eye
   potatoes, peeled
250 g (9 oz) green beans

250 g (9 oz) butter beans
juice of 1 lemon
4 tablespoons olive oil
4–6 tablespoons olive puree

Boil the potatoes in salted water and when cool, slice them. Blanch both the green and butter beans in boiling salted water, drain, and toss them with the lemon juice and half of the olive oil. Set aside.

Toss the potatoes and beans together in the remaining oil. Serve with large slivers of the warm poached fish, a generous dollop of the olive puree and some of the onion pickles.

CHAR-GRILLED TUNA STEAK AND RED CAPSICUM BUTTER

The Japanese are very choosy about tuna. They insist on only the perfect fish, since any bruising or battering means that the muscles of the creature would be separated, and the blocks they cut the back fillets from would be frayed and falling apart.

Tuna is best served raw or very rare, unless it is being used to flavour a mayonnaise or pasta sauce. A thick steak from the thick back fillet, lightly marked on a very hot barbecue, presents the fish at its best. The fattier flesh from the belly is best served raw with a vinaigrette and avocado salad.

We have served tuna with pesto, a hot crunchy witloof salad with pine nuts and snow peas, with a hot mustard mayonnaise, or various flavoured vinaigrettes like lime, ginger or soy sauce.

In this dish, as an acknowledgement of the Japanese delight in this fish, as well as a sharpening of the flavours, we have added sprouts of the white radish which the Japanese call daikon.

SERVES 4–6

THE RED CAPSICUM BUTTER (enough for 12 serves)

3 red capsicums

2 tablespoons capers in salt, rinsed

6 Golden Shallots, chopped

100 ml (3½ fl oz) white wine vinegar

freshly ground black pepper

350 g (12 oz) unsalted butter

Grill, peel and finely chop the capsicums, then puree with the capers and the shallots. Reduce the vinegar in a saucepan until there is only about 1 tablespoon left. Mix in all the other ingredients except the butter and cook until thick. Tip the cooked mixture into a bowl and whisk in the butter a little at a time. Strain through the medium grill of a food mill or blend in a food processor. Set aside to cool, stirring from time to time, until the butter is solid enough to roll. Roll the butter in aluminium foil that has been sprinkled with a little cold water, and refrigerate.

THE TUNA

4–6 x 200 g (7 oz) tuna steaks

juice of 2 limes

salt and pepper, to taste

4 tablespoons olive oil

2–3 limes, halved

1 punnet of white radish sprouts

Preheat the barbecue until very hot. Marinate the tuna steaks in the lime juice for 3–4 minutes. Season them quickly and mark both sides on the barbecue to produce a char-grill criss-cross pattern, then leave at the side of the barbecue plate for 2 minutes, depending on the thickness. Brush with olive oil and serve with a generous knob of the capsicum butter, half a lime and a pile of the sprouts.

STEAMED TROUT WITH LEMON GRASS AND SHIITAKE MUSHROOMS

Shiitake mushrooms have been cultivated in China and Japan for at least a thousand years. The Japanese name is a combination of the *shiia*, a hardwood tree on the trunk of which the fungus grows, and *take*, or mushroom. The whole process of cultivation is complex, needing 9 to 10 months and an ideal environment.

Nothing, though, can replace their distinctive flavour which we use in this dish to slightly sharpen a clear soup in which the trout are steamed.

To cook this dish you will need two bamboo steamers which will hold two bowls each and a pot or wok to sit them on.

SERVES 4

THE TROUT AND SOUP

1 knob of ginger root, grated

8 fresh shiitake mushrooms, sliced

1 root of lemon grass, pounded

1 small white radish, peeled, split and cut in eight pieces

400 ml (14 fl oz) Fish Stock (see page 23)

10 x 5 cm (2 in) squares of kombu (Japanese kelp)

4 lime leaves, dried or fresh

4 tablespoons dried binetto flakes, tied in muslin

juice of 1 lemon

4 small rainbow trout

½ bunch watercress leaves

Bring all the ingredients, except the trout and watercress leaves, to the boil and simmer for 15 minutes. Discard the binetto flakes.

Put each trout into a bowl and pour an equal amount of the liquid and the other ingredients, except the watercress, over them. Put the bowls in the steamers and stack one steamer on top of the other. Steam the trout, covered, for 12 minutes.

Using a sharp paring knife, skin the top side of each trout to reveal the pink flesh. You may like to skin the whole fish, but to some tastes the skin provides an accent to the whole flavour.

THE RICE

300 g (11 oz) jasmine rice

400 ml (14 fl oz) Chicken Stock (see page 23)

1 knob of ginger root, peeled and sliced

4 tablespoons sesame seeds

Cook the rice with the stock and ginger in a deep, covered pan for 20 minutes or until it is cooked. Five minutes before serving, put the watercress into the soup. Serve in individual bowls, sprinkled with the sesame seeds, to accompany the trout.

Buckwheat Blinis with Krill and Radish Sprouts   See page 96

Cos Lettuce Salad with Filetto   See page 94

ESCABECHE OF MACKEREL WITH SEED CRACKERS

This dish originated in Spain and has spread around the Mediterranean where it has a variety of names, all deriving, it seems, from the original Spanish. The Belgians also serve a version of it which they call escaveche. It is usually a fairly spicy dish and can be made from any number of small fish varieties. If preferred, use whiting, red mullet or sardines instead of the mackerel, or a mixture of each.

The dish can be prepared well in advance and kept in the refrigerator. In fact, since it is basically a marinade, storing will improve the compounding of the spicy flavours with the fish. If you are going to prepare it on the night, the warm fish will need marinating for at least 2 hours. It is a dish that will also stand on its own for a light summer lunch.

The recipe for the Seed Crackers is on page 56. Serve them whole or in large pieces on the side.

SERVES 4–6

THE MARINADE

1 orange	*1 teaspoon paprika*
2 tablespoons olive oil	*150 ml (5 fl oz) red wine vinegar*
4 hot red chillies, seeded and finely chopped	*1 red capsicum, grilled and cut into strips*
1 tablespoon coriander seeds, toasted and ground	*4 bay leaves*
1 teaspoon black peppercorns, cracked	*1 teaspoon sea salt*
	1 small red onion, sliced

Pare the zest from the orange, squeeze the juice and cut the peel into large chunks. Heat the olive oil in a pan, then fry the chillies and spices. Deglaze the pan with the vinegar and orange juice. Combine the remaining ingredients, including the orange zest and peel, and bring it to the boil. Simmer for 2 minutes or so, then set aside.

THE FISH

4–6 small mackerel, about 250 g (9 oz)	*1 L (1²/₃ pts) olive oil*
200 g (7 oz) flour, seasoned with salt and pepper	*1 bunch coriander leaves*

Fillet and carefully bone the fish. Dredge them in the flour, then deep fry in small batches in hot oil until sealed and lightly browned, but not cooked right through. Drain the fish and put them in a deep dish, then pour the marinade over. Let this cool, then refrigerate. Serve the fish with a little of the marinade and some coriander leaves on top.

GRILLED QUAIL WITH BEANS AND CURRY BUTTER

Although quail are bred for the table in Australia, they are considered game birds rather than poultry because in other parts of the world they are hunted.

They are a fine bird for grilling or roasting. In some parts of Europe they are grilled wrapped in leaves. In Asia they are more often marinated in some spicy mixture and then fried. Like squab, quail need to be served medium rare and are completely destroyed if cooked any longer.

SERVES 4–6

8 or 12 large quails

sea salt and freshly ground black pepper, to taste

½ teaspoon black cardarmom seeds, crushed

½ teaspoon ground cumin

a couple of pinches of cayenne pepper

1 knob ginger root, grated

juice of 2 limes

½ recipe Curry Butter (see page 81), chopped

100 ml (3½ fl oz) Chicken Stock (see page 23)

150 g (5 oz) green beans

150 g (5 oz) butter beans

½ bunch mint leaves

½ bunch coriander leaves

2–3 limes, halved

Split each bird down the back as if to spatchcock them and carefully remove the neck without tearing the breast skin. With a pair of scissors or nail snips, remove the backbone and the bones either side of the breastbone, leaving the breastbone intact. Tuck the wings behind where the neck was and make a small cut in the skin at the other end of the bird and tuck the feet through this. Sprinkle the birds with a generous amount of water. Press them flat with a cutlet bat or the flat side of a cleaver. Sprinkle with the spices and lime juice. Cover and set aside.

Heat the grill to maximum. Spread the flattened birds out on a grilling tray, season and sprinkle with pieces of curry butter. Save enough of the butter to serve a piece of it on each plate. Grill the quail for 5 minutes or until well coloured, but not cooked through. Transfer the birds to the warmed plates and keep warm. Deglaze the juices in the grilling tray with some of the hot chicken stock and pour the resulting sauce into a heated pan.

Quickly blanch the beans in boiling salted water and toss them directly into the pan with the sauce, giving them a good stir in the hot juices, but not cooking them much more.

Serve a pile of the beans alongside the quail. Put a slice of curry butter on each bird, sprinkle with the mint and coriander leaves and put half a lime on each plate.

THAI CHICKEN CURRY

This has been on the Brasserie's menu almost since it opened, and has become the top favourite of our patrons. If we took it off the menu there would be something of a consumer revolt, so it is likely to stay there until, if ever, the restaurant closes.

SERVES 8

THE CHICKEN

1 kg (2 lb 3 oz) chicken thighs

Debone the thighs, remove the skin and sinews, and chop the flesh coarsely.

THE CURRY SAUCE
4 tablespoons clarified butter
2 small onions, chopped
2 tablespoons Maesri curry paste
1 x 8 cm (3 in) piece ginger root, crushed
4 stalks lemon grass, split

1 x 500 g (18 oz) can of straw mushrooms, liquid reserved
12 dried shiitake mushrooms, soaked and drained
1 L (1²⁄₃ pts) coconut milk
6–8 lime leaves
150 ml (5 fl oz) sweet chilli sauce
100 ml (3½ fl oz) fish sauce

Heat the clarified butter to smoking hot and fry the onions with the curry paste. Add the ginger and lemon grass, and fry for a further 3 minutes.

Combine the mushrooms, including the liquid from the canned straw mushrooms, with the coconut milk and lime leaves, and pour onto the cooked onions and curry mixture. Add the chilli and fish sauces and simmer for 15 minutes. Remove the lemon grass and ginger root and discard them. Add the chopped chicken meat and simmer for 5 minutes, or until it is cooked.

THE GARNISH AND RICE
600 g (1¼ lb) jasmine rice
800 ml (28 fl oz) Chicken Stock (see page 23)

1 Lebanese cucumber, sliced
1 bunch coriander
4 tablespoons dried anchovies, fried

Wash the rice in plenty of water. Drain and cover it with the chicken stock, and bring this to the boil. Reduce the heat and simmer, covered, for 20 minutes.

Serve the chicken on the rice with a generous ladleful of the sauce on top, garnished with the cucumber slices, coriander sprigs and anchovies.

CHICKEN GIBLETS AND CHAR SIU WITH CELERY
AND KANGKONG

Char siu is the sticky pork that the Chinese use to stuff steamed pork buns, chung fun and rice noodle dim sim, or add to hot pot dishes. In this recipe it is served over the vegetables and chicken giblets. Kangkong, with its green leaf and hollow stems, looks a little like a strelitzia plant, but it is smaller and more delicate. It tastes and cooks rather like English spinach.

This dish is best made in a wok.

SERVES 4–6

THE CHAR SIU

250 g (9 oz) pork belly in one piece

100 ml (3½ fl oz) medium dry sherry/Chinese
 rice wine

50 ml (2 fl oz) thick soy sauce

50 ml (2 fl oz) thin soy sauce

1 tablespoon sesame oil

8 pieces star anise

1 tablespoon Sichuan pepper, toasted

1 x 4 cm (1½ in) piece ginger root, peeled
 and grated

Mix the ingredients together and marinate the pork overnight or for at least 8 hours. Roast on a cake rack in a preheated 180°C (350°F) oven for 30 minutes. You will need to baste throughout cooking, so sit the rack in a baking tray so the marinade does not burn on the oven bottom. Keep warm and reserve the marinade.

THE GIBLETS, LIVER AND VEGETABLES

200 g (7 oz) chicken giblets

100 ml (3½ fl oz) sherry

1 x 4 cm (1½ in) piece ginger root, peeled and
 grated

3–4 tablespoons grape seed oil

3 stalks celery, diagonally sliced

½ bunch spring onions, diagonally sliced

2 cloves garlic, smashed

200 g (7 oz) chicken livers, washed and
 trimmed

100 g (4 oz) chicken hearts, washed and
 trimmed

2 bunches kangkong, washed and cut in 10 cm
 (4 in) lengths

Split the giblets and remove any sinew. Marinate in the sherry and the ginger overnight.

Heat the grape seed oil in a wok until it is smoking hot and add the drained giblets, the celery, spring onions and garlic. Combine the giblet marinade with the char siu marinade. Stir fry for a couple of minutes. It is important to stir fry and not stew this dish, so you must keep lifting the cooking ingredients up and away from the centre of the wok where the juices will accumulate. Add the livers and stir fry for another minute or so. Add the hearts and the kangkong, pour in 50 ml (2 fl oz) of the reserved marinade and simmer for 2 minutes.

Spoon into bowls, top with the char siu which has been thinly sliced and drizzle a little of the wok juices over the top.

Note: It is a good idea to stir fry this recipe, one half at a time, to keep the wok at maximum heat. Return the first half before pouring in the marinade for the final simmer.

ROUGH STUFFED DUCK

This dish has not been on the menu of the Bayswater Brasserie, but it is one we have cooked for our own enjoyment for two Christmas dinners—one on either side of the Tasman. The first dinner was not a duck, but a goose, and the method worked just as well for both birds.

SERVES 4–6

THE DUCK

2 kg (4½ lb) duck

salt and pepper

Choose a duck with a large breast if possible, though these seem to be a scarce commodity in this part of the world. Clean the fat from the inside of the leg and remove the neck without splitting the skin. Chop up the neck and keep it for the braising dish. Rub the bird with salt and pepper inside and out.

THE VEGETABLE STUFFING

4 tablespoons olive oil

1 small orange yam, peeled

1 small head of celeriac, peeled

1 medium carrot, peeled

1 medium parsnip, peeled

2 medium zucchini, peeled

100 g (4 oz) okra, washed

10 spears asparagus, peeled if necessary

1 medium onion, peeled

4 bay leaves

4 tablespoons breadcrumbs

4 tablespoons melted butter

a few sprigs of sage, to taste

a few sprigs of thyme, to taste

salt and pepper, to taste

1 L (1²/₃ pts) Chicken or Duck Stock (see page 23)

Heat the olive oil in a roasting dish and brown the vegetables well, then roast in an oven preheated to 200°C (400°F) until cooked. Remember that some of them will cook at different speeds so take them out as they are done.

Choose a braising dish for the duck which will hold it without much room to spare. Let the roast vegetables cool until they can be handled, then split them lengthways into strips or chop them into large pieces. Make a bed of some of the root vegetables and two of the bay leaves in the bottom of the dish. Put the remaining bay leaves inside the duck.

Mix the rest of the vegetables with the breadcrumbs, melted butter, sage, thyme, salt and pepper. Be careful when making this stuffing mixture to keep the vegetable pieces as intact as possible. Stuff the duck with the vegetables and herbs, sew it up and truss it. Put the duck breast on the bed of vegetables in the pan and brown it at 240°C (475°F). When it is a rich dark brown, reduce the heat to 180°C (350°F) and take the duck out. Pour off any fat from the dish.

Meanwhile, bring the stock to the boil. If you do not have any stock, use plain water, but add raw chopped tomatoes to the bed of vegetables in the dish. Pour 4 cm (1½ in) of the hot stock into the bottom of the dish, replace the duck, and cook for 2 hours more. Throughout the braising, maintain the stock in the dish at the same level.

Remove the duck from the oven and cover it with foil to keep warm. Strain the braising liquid into a clean pan and skim it carefully. Correct the seasoning and reduce it down to a good, strong and tasty sauce.

To serve the duck, carve thin slices from the breast and halve the legs. Serve each portion with a substantial scoop of the vegetable stuffing and plenty of the sauce.

DUCKLING WITH TREE TOMATO CHUTNEY

Anyone who has cooked in European restaurants will appreciate the vast difference between the way the suppliers to those establishments treat game and poultry, and the barbaric treatment we mete out to ours. The beasts and birds arrive at European kitchen doors complete with fur and feathers and aged to perfection. And in what splendid variety they come too—woodsnipes, watersnipes, partridges, pheasants, pigeons, plump quail and squab, rich wild duck, rabbit, hare, wild boar and venison.

Not only is there a wonderful selection of wild species, but the domesticated versions bred for the table are exactly that—bred, fed and killed with the table in mind. The European birds are fed with the idea that what they eat will be converted into something that will delight those who eventually eat *them*. Ours, by contrast, seem to have been brought up on strips of cardboard.

Things are beginning to improve slightly, so when you choose poultry ask about the history of the birds you are being offered and go for the fresh, free-range, grain-fed birds. Particularly for this dish. It is a poultry dish that can be prepared in advance and reheated for serving.

SERVES 4

THE DUCKLINGS

2 x No. 14 (1.4 kg or 3 lb) ducklings

Prepare these the same way as those for the Rough Stuffed Duck recipe on page 111. These will weigh in at about 1.4 kilos a bird, so take the lower body weight into account when you cook them.

THE STUFFING

2 small sour apples, peeled and quartered

1 tablespoon chopped sage leaves

1 teaspoon thyme

1 clove garlic, crushed

500 ml (18 fl oz) apple cider

500 ml (18 fl oz) Chicken or Duck Stock (see page 23)

3 tablespoons cold butter, chopped

calvados or raspberry vinegar, to taste

4–6 tablespoons Tree Tomato Chutney (see page 168)

300 g (11 oz) broad beans, blanched

Stuff the ducklings with the combined apples, sage, thyme and garlic, sew them up and truss them. Set the birds in a roasting pan, breast up, with not too much room around them, and put in an oven preheated to 260°C (500°F) to colour. Once they are well coloured reduce the heat to 180°C (350°F), basting regularly with 250 ml (9 fl oz) of the cider. The whole cooking time will be about 1½ hours. When the birds are cooked set them aside to cool.

Deglaze the pan juices with the hot stock and pour the whole lot into a clean pan. Halve the ducklings with a pair of poultry shears and put the stuffing in the stock. Carefully remove the legs and breasts off the bone leaving the wing bones, and skin intact. Remove the bone at the body end of the leg, leaving the knuckle, then cut the knuckle off the drumstick. Trim the wing bone with the heel of a heavy knife. Pick out any bone splinters. With scissors, carefully separate the breasts from the legs keeping the skin intact. Make a parcel of each portion laying each breast over a leg.

Put all the bones and trimmings in the pan with the cooking liquids and bring it to the boil. A lot of fat will have come out of the ducklings so the stock will need to be carefully skimmed. Simmer this for 1 hour, skimming regularly, then strain through a sieve into a clean pan and reduce until it has plenty of flavour.

Before serving put the duckling parcels carefully into a roasting dish and baste each with about 50 ml (2 fl oz) of the reduced stock. Roast them at 220°C (425°F) for about 8 minutes or until the skins are crisp.

To finish the sauce, check the seasoning and bring it to the boil, then whisk a knob of cold butter through it and sprinkle with the calvados, which will echo the apple flavours of the duck, or the raspberry vinegar. Serve with a dollop of the tree tomato chutney, and broad beans which have been reheated in a little melted butter.

SPATCHCOCKED BABY CHICKEN WITH ASPARAGUS
AND STRACCHINO

For some curious reason the idea has spread around that spatchcock is some kind of small bird, perhaps a baby chicken. It is not at all unusual to be served a whole poussin which has been described on a menu as spatchcock. In fact, the word means a method of butchering a bird, of any kind, by splitting it down the back and flattening it so it can be quickly grilled. The word comes from an Irish dish in the eighteenth century called "dispatch-cock", which was a fowl split and grilled as an emergency meal.

The method suits any smallish bird that will grill. Given the right treatment beforehand and the right spices, oils, herbs or other flavours to burn on the skin, it can be a simple and delicious dish.

In this dish we suggest boning the spatchcocked baby chickens. This is not absolutely necessary, but if you can do it it will make things a little easier for your guests.

SERVES 4–6

THE CHICKENS

4–6 baby chickens

4 tablespoons olive oil

salt, to taste

100 g (4 oz) soft breadcrumbs

2 sprigs of rosemary

1 teaspoon freshly ground black pepper

4 tablespoons unsalted butter

200 ml (7 fl oz) Chicken Stock (see page 23)

Spatchcock the birds by cutting them carefully along the back, then pushing them down flat to break the hold of the bones. Remove the bones on either side of the backbone, the rib and the breastbone. Leave the leg bones and wings. Tuck the wings in behind the breast and insert the leg ends in the skin at the back of the bird. Sprinkle with cold water and press down again with a cutlet bat or a small cutting board.

Heat the olive oil in a pan, season the birds on both sides and seal them in the hot oil starting with the skin side. Arrange the birds in a roasting dish skin side up. Sprinkle them with breadcrumbs, rosemary leaves, and black pepper, and dot them with the butter. Heat the chicken stock and spoon a little into the roasting dish to provide moisture during cooking, but keep it off the breaded birds. Cook the birds in an oven preheated to 220°C (425°F) for about 10 minutes or until they are brown.

THE ASPARAGUS

3 bunches asparagus

3 tablespoons unsalted butter

200 g (7 oz) stracchino, cut in strips

4 eggs, hard boiled and chopped

75 g (3 oz) prosciutto, sliced very thinly

Clean and peel the asparagus and blanch them in bundles, spear end up, in boiling salted water until they are cooked but still crisp. Refresh in cold water and drain. Cut the spears on an angle into pieces about 4 cm (1½ in) in length, so they are the same length as the stracchino strips. They should look like short, tubular penne pasta.

If you have timed things well the chickens will be just cooked. Remove them from the oven and let them rest in a warm place for at least 5 minutes.

Heat the butter to foaming in a heavy-based pan and toss the asparagus briefly to coat the pieces and warm them for serving. Combine the warmed asparagus with the stracchino in a bowl.

Arrange the birds in the centre of the plates and spoon the asparagus and cheese mixture around them. Moisten the asparagus with the stock from the chickens and sprinkle it with the chopped egg and proscuitto slices. Keep the stock off the breadcrumbs which you will want to keep crisp.

TWICE-COOKED SQUAB WITH BURGHUL AND LENTIL SALAD

Squabs are young pigeons bred for the table rather than hunted, so they are considered to be poultry not game. They are usually four weeks old when killed and just slightly smaller than a baby chicken or "poussin". The flesh is slightly red in colour and like quail, the meat is usually better served medium rare. However, for this dish it is cooked through.

Burghul or cracked wheat is a delicious alternative to rice and pasta. It originated in the Middle East where it is used in soups and stews, or cooked as rice is cooked for a pilav. The harissa used to flavour the squab also comes from the Middle East and is a puree of small chilli peppers, cayenne, garlic oil and various herbs with dried mint or verbena leaves. If you cannot find harissa, a smaller amount of sambal will do as a substitute.

This is not a hot dish—the birds and salad are served at room temperature—so it is might be best as a summer dinner.

SERVES 4–6

THE SALAD
3 tablespoons butter
1 small red Spanish onion
200 g (7 oz) brown lentils, soaked
salt and pepper, to taste
400 ml (14 fl oz) Chicken Stock (see page 23)

200 g (7 oz) burghul wheat, washed
4 small zucchini, quartered lengthways
3 tablespoons olive oil
75 g (3 oz) blanched almonds, roasted and salted

Heat the butter in a saucepan and saute the onion until it is translucent. Drain the lentils and add them to the onion. Cover them with fresh water, season with salt and pepper, and simmer for 20–30 minutes, or until the lentils are tender but not mushy.

Meanwhile bring the chicken stock to the boil and simmer the burghul in it for about 15 minutes or until it is tender. Saute the zucchini in olive oil for 2–3 minutes. Drain the lentils and onion, season the burghul and mix them carefully together with the zucchini and almonds in a large dish. Set aside to cool until warm.

THE SQUABS

1 medium red Spanish onion
1 clove garlic
1 small knob of ginger root, grated
½ bunch parsley
4 teaspoons harissa or chilli paste
2 teaspoons ground cumin
2 teaspoons ground coriander

1 teaspoon ground black pepper
1 tablespoon sea salt
1 small pinch of saffron threads
4–6 squabs, washed and dried inside and out
zest of 2 lemons
150 ml (5 fl oz) Chicken Stock (see page 23)
250 ml (9 fl oz) clarified butter

Puree the onion, garlic, ginger, parsley, harissa and all the spices except the salt and saffron. Rub the squabs inside and out with the salt and the spice puree. Set them aside for at least 30 minutes.

Put the lemon zest and the saffron threads into the chicken stock and bring it to the boil. Set this aside to combine.

Heat a knob of butter in a heavy-based or enamel-lined pan. Colour the squabs on each side and add the saffron liquid. Reduce the liquid until it is quite syrupy, turning the birds regularly. This should only take 4–5 minutes. Retain the liquid and halve the birds through the breast and backbone.

Fry the squab halves in the clarified butter in a deep pan until they are golden brown on each side. Serve with a pile of the salad and a spoonful of yoghurt or sour cream.

WARM GRILLED BEEF AND ROAST TOMATOES

This is a substantial main dish, but one that can quite easily be served on a warm summer night. It is also a fine picnic dish and one that can be prepared in advance, so the cook can also enjoy eating it in a relaxed frame of mind.

The tomatoes in this dish should be a good firm variety. The Italian plum tomatoes will do very well, or the pear shaped "acid free" species. As a general rule, although it does not matter too much here as they are going to be cooked, tomatoes need time to recover their flavour from cold storage. They should never be served chilled unless for some reason you want to dispense with their flavour.

SERVES 4–6

THE BEEF
1 kg (2 lb 3 oz) fillet of beef or ox
sea salt and black pepper, to taste

1 L (1²/₃ pts) Veal Stock (see page 22),
reduced to 500 ml (18 fl oz)
2 hot chillies, seeded

Trim the meat of all fat, membrane and silver skin, and season it well with the sea salt and black pepper. Bring the stock to the boil with the seeded chillies and let it simmer for 2–3 minutes. Throw the beef onto a hot barbecue and seal it to a crisp all round. Put the beef into a container which can be tightly sealed, and pour the hot stock over to completely cover it. Set it aside to cool until warm.

THE TOMATOES
200 ml (7 fl oz) olive oil
8–12 large ripe tomatoes, washed and dried

salt and pepper, to taste
100 g (4 oz) soft breadcrumbs

Heat the olive oil in a roasting pan, then add the tomatoes, placing them with the side opposite the stem facing down. Brown them and turn over. Season with the salt and pepper, sprinkle with the crumbs and baste each tomato with some of the oil. Roast in an oven preheated to 180°C (350°F) for about 10 minutes or until they are cooked. Set aside ready to serve.

THE PESTO (enough for 400 g or 14 oz)
3 bunches green basil leaves
100 g (4 oz) roasted pine nuts

100 g (4 oz) freshly grated Parmesan cheese
sea salt and pepper, to taste
400 ml (14 fl oz) extra virgin olive oil

Mix all the ingredients together and pass through the fine grill of a mincer, or quickly blend in a food processor. The mixture should be a paste and you should take care not to let too much air get to the leaves. Store in a jar, covered with a little of the oil.

Serve 2 tomatoes on each plate with 3–4 5 mm (¼ in) slices of the beef. Put a tablespoon of pesto on top of the tomatoes and drizzle some over the beef. Serve with a good crisp salad and generous slices of crunchy country bread.

Note: Pesto will keep refrigerated; just make sure there is always a layer of oil on top of it. It is a very useful summer garnish and can be used as sauce for pasta or pizza. It should never be cooked.

BOILED BEEF FILLET AND AUTUMN VEGETABLES

The traditional name for this dish is Fillet Ficelle, or fillet on a string. It is a distant relative of that medieval family of boiled courses which once formed an important part of any banquet. Fish, meat, offal, game birds and sometimes whole sheep or goats were boiled for a long period in a broth of stock and vegetables, and the whole lot served together. Some of these old dishes evolved into soups and some into stews like the traditional Pot au Feu. They also have in common the rugged condiments that went with them, like coarse salt, pounded horseradish and grainy mustards.

In this particular dish the meat is not cooked for long so we use a tender cut. The broth will need to have a full and vigorous flavour before the meat is poached in it. We have added some field mushrooms to the stock to enhance the flavour and, if you want to go further than that, you can also add tomatoes. In any case these additions should simmer in the stock for a lengthy time and be strained out before the vegetables and meat are added.

SERVES 4–6

THE POACHING STOCK
3 L (5 pts) Veal Stock (see page 22), reduced
  by a half

6 large field mushrooms
2 bay leaves

Bring the cold stock to the boil with the whole mushrooms and bay leaves. Let it simmer for 20 minutes or so, then strain out the mushrooms and bay leaves. Set it aside to cool.

THE VEGETABLES AND MEAT
2 medium chokos, peeled and cut in quarters
2 or 3 small leeks, well washed and cut in
  quarters
1 head of celeriac, cut in eight pieces
4–6 medium Jerusalem artichokes, scrubbed

10 baby carrots, scrubbed
10 baby turnips, scrubbed
4–6 x 250 g (9 oz) beef fillets, trimmed of fat,
  silver skin and membrane

Separately cook each of the different vegetables until tender in some of the stock. With the exception of the leeks, all the vegetables should be started in cold stock. Keep the vegetables in a warm dish in the oven. Strain the remaining stock and juices back into the pan for poaching the meat.

Bring the poaching stock to the boil. Tie a piece of string around the middle of each fillet and hang them from a wooden spoon fitted across the top of the poaching pot. It is important that the meat can hang down into the boiling stock without touching the bottom of the pot. Simmer the beef for 7–8 minutes depending on the thickness. Lift them out and rest in the oven for 5 minutes with the vegetables.

THE CREAMY HORSERADISH
150 ml (5 fl oz) cream
1 tablespoon freshly ground black pepper and
    sea salt, mixed

2 tablespoons grated horseradish
pinch of grated nutmeg

Unless you have the fortitude to put up with streaming eyes and nose while you grate your own, use pre-prepared horseradish for this.

Bring the cream to the boil, add the salt and pepper, horseradish and nutmeg, simmer for 2 minutes, then pass through a fine sieve. Set aside.

To serve, cut each piece of meat through the middle and place in the centre of a deep dish. Arrange the vegetables around the meat and pour a generous ladle of broth over them. Sprinkle the creamy horseradish over the vegetables.

LAMB CUTLETS WITH OLIVE BREAD AND EGGPLANT

Sailors, it is said, once used to take olive bread to sea with them because the oil kept it fresh and the olives kept their flavour. True or not, the bread is so good it deserves some mythology, and it is not difficult to imagine eating it while afloat on the balmy and blue Mediterranean.

In this dish the quantity of lamb is deliberately kept small so as to give the three components of the dish an equal part. It can also make a delicious summer lunch as well as a main course. The olive bread complements all sorts of things like Tomatoes Provençale, or slices of cured ocean trout, for a splendid picnic.

SERVES 4–6
THE OLIVE BREAD (8–10 serves)
4 cloves garlic, peeled and finely chopped
4 tablespoons olive oil
2 tablespoons yeast
300 ml (11 fl oz) water

475 g (17 oz) plain flour
1 tablespoon salt
200 g (7 oz) Onion Puree (see page 128)
1 tablespoon rosemary leaves
500 g (18 oz) black olives, pitted and chopped

Fry the garlic in half the olive oil until it is a golden brown. Dissolve the yeast in the water. Make a well in the flour, add the salt and form a dough. Roll it out into a rectangle.

Spread the onion puree over one half, leaving a clear 1 cm (¼ in) around the edge. Spread the rosemary leaves and the chopped olives on top of the puree and sprinkle with the garlic. Moisten the clean edge of the dough with cold water, then fold the plain side over, and press firmly together along the edge. Brush the loaf with the remaining olive oil and set it aside for 1 hour or until doubled in size.

Bake in an oven preheated to 220°C (425°F) for 15–20 minutes—it should be quite dark in colour—then rest the bread. When ready to serve, remove the end and cut into 2.5 cm (1 in) slices.

THE EGGPLANTS
2 large eggplants, halved lengthways
2 tablespoons salt
1 x 150 g (5 oz) Fromage Fermier goat's
  cheese, grated

salt and freshly ground black pepper, to taste
75 ml (3 fl oz) olive oil
2 cinnamon sticks, split

Salt the eggplants and let them stand for 40 minutes. Bake flat-side down until soft in an oven preheated to 180°C (350°F). When they are cool enough to handle, roughly dice them and mix with the goat's cheese, then season. Grease an ovenproof dish with a little of the olive oil and spoon in the mixture, carefully pressing the cinnamon sticks into the top. Sprinkle with some more olive oil and return to the oven for 20 minutes. Let the cooked dish cool until warm before serving.

THE LAMB
4–6 x 4-bone lamb racks
salt and pepper, to taste

a few sprigs of rosemary leaves
1 or 2 tablespoons chilli oil, or to taste
125 g (4 fl oz) olive oil

Rub the lamb with the salt, pepper, rosemary leaves and chilli oil. Heat the olive oil in a roasting pan, seal the meat, then roast for 8 minutes in an oven pre-heated to 220°C (425°F). Rest the lamb for 4–5 minutes before serving, then cut each rack down the centre to make 2 double chops. Serve a slice of the bread and a pile of the eggplant alongside the lamb.

ROLLED STUFFED LAMB LOIN AND WARM POTATO SALAD

This cut of meat comes from the saddle of the lamb and in New Zealand it is called the two middle loins. These are joined together by the backbone. You will need one loin for each serve of this dish

Ask your butcher to prepare this cut from the leg end of the loin since the shoulder end is split by a piece of sinew. Ask for all the meat that covers the bones, including the apron or flap at the bottom and the fillet from the underside of the cut. The flap is used to cover both the stuffing and the loin, and to keep them moist during cooking. You will also need the bones.

Also ask the butcher to remove the surplus fat. Depending on the age and origin of the creature there may be a considerable amount of this. The musty taste that is often associated with sheep meat comes almost entirely from the fat and the leaner you can make your lamb cut, the sweeter tasting it will be.

SERVES 4–6

THE SAUCE

the bones from the loins

1 small onion, roughly chopped

12 purple eshallots

2 cloves garlic

2 medium carrots, roughly chopped

3 sticks celery, roughly chopped

800 ml (28 fl oz) Veal Stock (see page 22)

2 bay leaves

salt and pepper, to taste

Roast the bones with the vegetables in the oven until they are quite brown, then scrape everything into a pan. Just cover with the stock, tuck in the bay leaves, season and bring to the boil. Simmer for 3 hours, skimming off the fat regularly.

To make the sauce, strain off the solids, and reduce the liquid until it is dark brown and quite strong in flavour, then set aside until serving.

THE STUFFING

1 bunch mint

½ bunch each red and green basil leaves

150 ml (5 fl oz) olive oil

150 g (5 oz) pine nuts

150 g (5 oz) raisins

1 tablespoon sea salt

1 tablespoon freshly ground black pepper

Coarsely chop the mint and basil leaves. Heat the oil in a pan and saute the pine nuts until they are dark brown. Tip the nuts into a bowl and mix with the mint, basil and raisins, and season. Pass the mixture through the fine grill of a mincer and set aside to cool.

THE LAMB LOINS

4–6 x 250 g (9 oz) prepared loins

salt and pepper, to taste

150 ml (5 fl oz) olive oil

2 large onions, peeled and thickly sliced

1 sprig of rosemary

2 bay leaves

Spoon about 3 tablespoons of stuffing onto the fat side of each loin, hard up against the lean meat. Press the fillet into the stuffing, then spread a little more along the flap. Stretch the flap right around the stuffing and the loin, and tie it into a roll with twine. Do not tie it too tightly.

Season the loins with salt and pepper, and brown them in a heavy-based pan in some of the olive oil. Place the browned loins on the onion slices in a roasting pan and tuck in the rosemary and bay leaves, sprinkle with the rest of the olive oil and roast in an oven preheated to 220°C (425°F) for 20 minutes. Cover with foil and let them rest for a good 10 minutes.

THE WARM SALAD

3 tablespoons white wine vinegar

salt and pepper, to taste

1 bunch chives, chopped

125 ml (4 fl oz) olive oil

4–6 sweet potatoes

3–4 tablespoons olive oil

12 red chats potatoes

a sprig of mint

Begin by making the vinaigrette. Mix together the vinegar, seasoning and chives, then whisk in the 125 ml (4 fl oz) olive oil in a steady stream.

Colour the sweet potatoes in the 3–4 tablespoons of olive oil and roast them until they are firm but cooked right through. Cut them into thirds and keep them warm. At the same time, boil the red potatoes in salted water with the sprig of mint. Slice the red potatoes, mix with the sweet, and while they are both still on the hot side of warm, souse them with the vinaigrette.

Reheat the sauce and coat the plates. Cut the loins into three and arrange them on one side of the plate, with the salad on the other.

SPICED FILLET OF BEEF WITH MASHED POTATOES, PANCETTA AND SHALLOTS

In North Africa cooks roll beef in salt and a variety of spices, then air-dry it to make the flavouring for a casserole called Tagine, named after the cooking pot it is made in.

The spices the beef fillet is rolled in for this dish are used partly to flavour the meat and partly to add texture to the dish. Using spices instead of breadcrumbs for texture is also a pleasant alternative for frying fish, particularly an oily fish like the sardine. They are marvellous coated with crunchy spices, fried, and served with a pickled lemon.

The fillet in this dish should be cooked until it is crisp on the outside and rare inside. To achieve this you will need plenty of heat in the pan and a reasonable depth of oil. The finished meat will have a slightly piquant crust.

Spiced Fillet of Beef with Mashed Potatoes, Pancetta and Shallots   See page 122

Duckling with Tree Tomato Chutney   See page 112

124

SERVES 4–6

THE MASHED POTATOES

*400 g (14 oz) Pontiac potatoes,
    peeled and halved*

100 g (4 oz) butter, chopped

100 ml (3½ fl oz) hot milk

sea salt and freshly ground white pepper

Cook the potatoes in salted water until tender when tested with a very sharp knife. Drain off the water and let the potatoes steam dry in the pan, being careful not to burn the bottom. Push the potatoes through a sieve with a wooden spoon or masher. Stir the butter and the milk through the mashed potato to make a smooth creamy mix. Season and keep warm and covered.

THE SAUCE

20 Pickled Shallots (see page 63)

20 thin slices of pancetta

*1 L (1²/₃ pts) Veal Stock (see page 22),
    reduced to 300 ml (11 fl oz)*

Simmer the pickled shallots and pancetta in the reduced stock, skimming regularly for 15 minutes.

THE FILLETS

1 tablespoon coriander seeds

1 tablespoon cumin seeds

1 tablespoon black peppercorns

4–6 x 200 g (7 oz) beef fillet steaks

200 ml (7 fl oz) clarified butter

Toast all the spices and grind them together, in either a mortar or an electric grinder, until very fine. Roll the fillets in the spices, pressing them firmly into the meat. Heat at least 1 cm (¼ in) clarified butter in a heavy-based pan until very hot, then add the fillets. Saute until they are dark brown and crusty on the outside and rare inside.

Serve the fillets with a large scoop of potato on the side. Dress the potato with slices of the pancetta and a ladleful of the sauce it was cooked in.

BREADED VEAL CUTLETS WITH TOMATO AND
AVOCADO SALAD

S oggy chicken Kiev, fatty lamb cutlets from the butcher and sinewy schnitzels
have given breaded meats something of a bad name. That is a great pity,
since breadcrumbs and spices can deliver a deliciously flavoured pink meat,
with a robust texture, to the table in a way that no other method can.

First, though, get the crumbs right. For frying you must use the soft white
crumbs, not the brown toasted ones. These toasted ones are fine for scattering
on top of a dish as a finish, but they are already cooked and will simply lose
any virture they began with if you cook them again.

Make the crumbs for this dish from stale white bread. Cut off the crusts
and push the bread through a coarse metal sieve, or process in a food processor.
These will keep for a day or two in the refrigerator.

SERVES 4–6

THE SALAD

*350 ml (12 fl oz) Veal Stock (see page 22),
reduced to 175 ml (6 fl oz)*

4 large ripe tomatoes, sliced

2–3 avocados, sliced

½ bunch red and green basil leaves, chopped

100 ml (3½ fl oz) extra virgin olive oil

4 tablespoons balsamic vinegar

sea salt and ground black pepper, to taste

Bring the veal stock to the boil. Arrange the tomato slices on a tray and top
with the avocados and basil. Sprinkle with the oil, vinegar, salt and pepper.

THE CUTLETS

4–6 x 200 g (7 oz) veal cutlets

1 tablespoon rosemary

1 tablespoon thyme

1 tablespoon basil

4 tablespoons grated Parmesan cheese

150 g (5 oz) soft breadcrumbs

2 eggs

4 tablespoons olive oil

4 tablespoons butter

Trim the cutlets of any fat and scrape the bones. Mix the herbs, Parmesan and
breadcrumbs together. Beat the eggs well and dip the cutlets in them, then press
them into the crumb and herb mix, covering them well. Set aside in a cool place
to allow the coating to fix.

To cook the cutlets, heat the olive oil to smoking in a heavy-based pan,
and add the butter in pieces. Saute the cutlets for 3–4 minutes or until both sides
are crisp and golden brown.

Serve some veal stock onto each plate, lift the salad from the tray onto
each plate beside the cutlet, and make sure each gets plenty of dressing.

BORLOTTI BEAN STEW WITH LAMB SHANKS AND BABY TURNIPS

Bean stews of various kinds are favourite dishes in France and the Middle East. The best known French versions are the cassoulets from Languedoc which get their creamy colour from haricot beans. In this dish we follow the Middle Eastern preference for lamb, using the shank, a much despised but wonderful part of the beast.

The finished shank is a marvellously sticky and gelatinous thing, but to achieve that, it has to be cooked until the meat is almost falling from the bone and all the collagen transformed to gelatine.

You may, depending on the delicacy of your guests, serve the shank either on the bone, or with the bone discarded and the meat chopped into chunks.

SERVES 4–6

THE SHANKS

1 L (1²/₃ pts) Veal Stock (see page 22)

olive oil

4–6 lamb shanks

2 medium carrots, roughly chopped

2 large leeks, roughly chopped

6 sticks celery, roughly chopped

2 small onions, roughly chopped

100 g (4 oz) pancetta in 1 piece, skinned

2 bay leaves

freshly ground black pepper

Bring the stock to the boil. Heat the oil in a heavy-based ovenproof casserole and colour the shanks well. Add the vegetables, pancetta, bay leaves and black pepper, and pour in the boiling stock. Skim well.

Braise in the oven at 200°C (400°F) for 2½–3 hours until the flesh moves easily away from the bone. Baste the shanks throughout the cooking.

Transfer the meat and vegetables to a colander to drain. Strain the cooking liquid into a clean pot which has enough room to hold the meat and vegetables, and skim thoroughly. Check the liquid for seasoning and correct if necessary.

THE BEANS AND TURNIPS

24 baby turnips

400 g (14 oz) fresh borlotti beans, shelled

4 tablespoons virgin olive oil

juice of ½ a lemon

½ bunch parsley, chopped

Peel the turnips, leaving a little of their green tops. Blanch the turnips and beans separately in salted water, refresh in cold water and set aside.

To serve, chop the meat from the shanks, cut the pancetta into batons about 4 cm (1½ in) long and ½ cm (¼ in) thick. Heat the meat and all the vegetables in the stock, and serve in deep dishes with forks and soup spoons. Sprinkle each dish with the olive oil, lemon juice, and parsley. If you like, large croutons can be a useful addition.

CALF'S LIVER WITH ONION PUREE AND
HASH BROWN POTATOES

C alf's liver, the elite among offal, is fine and tender with a particularly delicate flavour. The most usual and the simplest way to cook the liver is to saute it, the method we have used here. The best known French version of this is from Lyon, where it is served with a garnish of sauteed onions sharpened with a little vinegar. Our dish belongs to this family.

SERVES 4

THE CALF'S LIVER

600 g (1½ lb) calf's liver, cleaned

salt and pepper, to taste

olive oil

2 tablespoons unsalted butter

flour, for dusting

1 L (1²/₃ pts) Veal Stock (see page 22), reduced to 200 ml (7 fl oz)

½ bunch parsley, chopped

THE ONION PUREE

5 medium Spanish onions

150 ml (5 fl oz) balsamic vinegar

4 tablespoons brown sugar

salt and pepper, to taste

1 teaspoon black mustard seeds

2 tablespoons unsalted butter

THE HASH BROWNS

see recipe, page 36

Put all the ingredients for the onion puree into a pan, except the butter, and simmer steadily for 40 minutes or until the onions are very soft. Puree the mixture, then pass it through a coarse sieve. Check the seasoning and adjust if necessary. If the puree is too liquid, return it to a clean saucepan and cook gently until reduced to a thick puree. Keep warm.

Cut the cleaned calf's liver on an angle into 5 cm (¼ in) slices, season, sprinkle with olive oil, then leave in a cool place while preparing the hash browns.

Heat enough olive oil to cover the bottom of a large, heavy-based pan, then add 2 tablespoons of unsalted butter. Dredge the liver slices in flour, shaking off any excess, then quickly saute them on both sides. Transfer to a warm oven. Deglaze the pan with the veal stock, add the parsley and cook for 2 minutes more. Just before serving, whisk the other 2 tablespoons of butter into the hot onion puree.

Serve the liver stacked on one side of the plate, moistened with the sauce. Arrange the crisp hash browns alongside with a generous dollop of onion puree.

POACHED VEAL TONGUE WITH CHICKEN BREAST AND SPINACH AND POLENTA TOAST

According to Waverley Root, the Roman legions conquered the world on polenta, and it was the Etruscans who introduced them to this finely ground maize flour. Polenta is used in cakes and biscuits, to make gnocchi, as a pudding, and grilled, fried or toasted as a base for savoury dishes.

SERVES 4–6

THE POLENTA
500 ml (18 fl oz) water
100 g (4 oz) polenta

½ teaspoon salt
50 g (2 oz) unsalted butter
walnut oil

Bring the water to the boil and add the polenta and salt in a steady stream, whisking all the time. Simmer for about 30 minutes, stirring it constantly away from the sides with a wooden spoon. Stir the butter through the cooked mixture, then spread it out on an oiled tray to cool, cover and refrigerate.

THE MEATS
2–3 pickled veal tongues, cooked in a Court Boullion (see page 89)

4–6 large chicken breasts, skinned
200 ml (7 fl oz) Chicken Consomme (see page 23)

Peel the tongues while they are hot. Put the chicken breasts in a tightly covered pan and just cover them with the chicken consome. Simmer gently, covered, for 3–4 minutes, turning to make sure they cook through and checking the heat so they do not boil at any stage. Remove from the heat and keep warm in the cooking juices.

To cook the polenta, cut it into 4–6 squares about the size of a bread slice, then halve each piece diagonally. Brush with the walnut oil and grill both sides until crispy brown. Keep them warm.

THE VEGETABLES
2 bunches English spinach
4 tablespoons unsalted butter

100 g (4 oz) black olives, pitted
4–6 tablespoons Thelma's Plum Sauce (see page 170)

Steam the spinach in ½ cm (¼ in) of water in a covered pan, until limp. Refresh with cold water, wring out and roughly chop. Heat the butter in a heavy-based pan and toss the olives and spinach through it until warm.

Serve a pile of the spinach-olive mixture over 2 pieces of polenta pushed together in the centre of each plate. Halve each chicken breast, split each tongue and arrange them around the spinach toast. Serve a dollop of Thelma's Plum Sauce on the side.

CORNED BRISKET WITH CREAMED ONIONS AND CHOKOS

The brisket of beef comes from the breast of the beast. Said like that it cuts something of a dash, but sadly this is a cut much despised for eating. It is generally reserved for stock or bouillon and when it is cooked in its own right it is most often boiled.

It probably earns its bad reputation by being widely abused in the cooking since it is a cut that must be cooked slowly over a long period. Marbled with fat, brisket cooked properly is wonderfully gelatinous. Corned, it is certainly a superior cut to the more commonly used silverside.

A superb recipe given to us by a friend involves rubbing the brisket with spice and tomatoes and sealing it in foil to cook for several hours. It is then cut into generous slices and barbecued.

SERVES 8

THE CORNED BRISKET

1.5 kg (3lb 5 oz) brisket of beef

Choose a cut which has the least fat, and bone it. Use the brining and cooking method given for Corned Beef on page 41. It is best left to sit in the court bouillon it was cooked in and served warm.

THE VEGETABLES

8 chokos
1 kg (2lb 3 oz) green onions or bunching onions
100 ml (3½ fl oz) clarified butter
250 ml (9 fl oz) Chicken Stock (see page 23)

150 ml (5 fl oz) cream
2 tablespoons mustard
salt and pepper, to taste
½ bunch parsley, chopped

Peel and stone the chokos, then steam them for 40 minutes until tender. Saute the onions in the clarified butter for 15 minutes or until they are clear and without any colour. Add the chokos and simmer for a further 2 minutes. Pour in the clear stock, bring to the boil and simmer for 5 minutes more.

In the meantime, bring the cream to the boil and add it and the mustard to the chokos and onions. Take off the heat, season with salt and pepper, and add the parsley. Serve the creamy vegetables alongside 2 or 3 generous slices of the beef.

Note: This recipe is great reheated the next day.

Pudding

Strictly speaking, nothing in this part of the book is a pudding, which to use the word in its original meaning is something—meat or fruit—boiled in a pastry casing bound with suet. Steak and kidney, and plum puddings are typical of the species. Nowadays pudding is the term for that group of cakes, ices and sweets that get served after a main meal, and in many places are still called desserts.

In the Brasserie repertoire a pudding often stands as a dish in its own right, eaten later in the afternoon or as a supper. Many of the Bayswater regulars drop in at those times for some of the cakes offered here. Puddings are and ought to be rich and almost all in this chapter are, so treat them with caution and offer them in moderate portions.

The Bayswater Brasserie is proud of its puddings, and much of their success is due to Christopher Walton. We are happy to offer here a range of some of the most successful from its menu.

Note: Gelatine, which is required in several of the following puddings can be purchased in different forms, frequently in sheets or in powder. As different forms provide different quantities of gelatine, the following is a guide to comparable weights in grams.
3 level teaspoons gelatine = 10 g
10 sheets oetker gelatine = 17 g
6 sheets goldweib gelatine = 17 g
5 level teaspoons powdered gelatine = 17 g

Bayswater Brasserie Book of Food

BAKED APPLES, GINGER AND CARAMEL

There is something very nostalgic about baked apples, a winter treat remembered from childhood perhaps. Certainly there are few puddings that seem so suited to that time of the year.

For this dish we use Golden Delicious apples. You can use other varieties, but these do not seem to break up so much. The fruit is much better peeled. Some old recipes just call for the apple skin to be split with a sharp knife, but however it is dealt with, cooked apple skin is not good to eat.

SERVES 8

16 apples (Golden Delicious), peeled and cored
a pinch of ground ginger
a pinch of ground cloves
a pinch of ground nutmeg
250 g (9 oz) mixed dried fruit

600 g (18 oz) caster sugar
575 ml (20 fl oz) orange juice
juice and zest of 1 lemon, chopped
2 tablespoons crystallised ginger, chopped
200 g (7 oz) almonds, blanched

Add the spices to the dried fruit and stuff the apples. Melt the caster sugar and cook until caramelised. When it is golden brown, add the orange juice, lemon juice and zest, crystallised ginger and almonds. Bring to the boil and pour over the apples. Bake them uncovered, basting and turning occasionally, for 1½ hours in an oven preheated to 150°C (300°F). Serve with the cooking liquid poured over and creme fraiche.

APRICOT RICOTTA CAKE

This dish was inspired by a classic baked Tuscan cheesecake. The original was garnished with crystallised green and red fruit, but having a personal prejudice about that combination, on cakes or anything else, we have left them out of this dish and added dried apricots.

SERVES 8

1 tablespoon soft butter
2 tablespoons raw sugar
75 g (3 oz) caster sugar
7 eggs, separated
600 g (1¼ lb) ricotta cheese
zest and juice of 3 oranges

125 g (4 oz) mixed peel
125 g (4 oz) plain flour
pinch of salt
250 g (9 oz) dried apricots, chopped
3 tablespoons sliced almonds
icing sugar, for dusting

132

Brush a 25 cm (10 in) springform tin with a tablespoon of soft butter and coat with raw sugar, tipping out the excess.

Cream the caster sugar and egg yolks together. Fold through the ricotta, zest and orange juice, peel, flour, salt and apricots. Whisk the egg whites to soft peaks and carefully fold into the cake mixture. Fill the tin three-quarters full and sprinkle with the sliced almonds. Bake in an oven preheated to 180°C (350°F) for 60-70 minutes.

Let the cake cool in the tin for 10 minutes. Dust with icing sugar and serve with some creme fraiche.

CHOCOLATE CARAMEL MOUSSE CAKE ON AN ALMOND BISCUIT

This is a rich summer pudding which you really should, perhaps, only eat once a summer or, to be very indulgent, twice.

SERVES 8 OR MAKES 2 CAKES

THE ALMOND BISCUITS	
100 g (4 oz) butter	*75 g (3 oz) plain flour*
90 g (3 oz) sugar	*2 eggs*
2 tablespoons ground almonds	*½ teaspoon baking powder*

Beat the butter and sugar together. Add the almonds, flour, eggs and baking powder, and mix well. Spread the mixture on a tray lined with silicon paper, then bake in an oven preheated to 180°C (350°F) for 20 minutes or until brown. Cool and cut into circles with a 23 cm (9 in) cake tin.

THE CHOCOLATE MOUSSE	
300 g (11 oz) chocolate couverture	*60 ml (2½ fl oz) oil*
	500 ml (18 fl oz) double cream

Melt the chocolate and oil, then let cool slightly. Fold the cream into the chocolate mix. Put the biscuits into 2 cake tins and pour the mousse over. Set aside in the fridge.

THE CARAMEL	
250 g (9 oz) sugar	*250 g (9 fl oz) water*
	100 g (3½ fl oz) extra water

Bring the sugar and water to the boil, and cook until it turns to dark caramel. Add the extra water and cool. This recipe makes double the quantity required and the excess can be stored at room temperature for several weeks.

THE CARAMEL MOUSSE

3 eggs, separated

575 ml (1 pt) cream

1 vanilla bean, split

7 sheets gelatine, soaked in cold water

Whisk the egg yolks and 200 ml (7 fl oz) caramel together. Heat the cream with the vanilla bean, then pour the yolks and caramel over.

Cook, stirring continuously until boiling. This stage is reached when the mixture evenly coats the back of a wooden spoon. Stir in the gelatine sheets, then strain and cool over ice.

Whisk the egg whites until stiff, then fold into the custard. Pour on top of the chocolate mousse and set in the refrigerator.

Note: The almond biscuit can be made in advance and stored in a sealed tin. They can be used as a base for mousse or layered with fruit and butter cream.

BAKED LEMON TART

The French, Italians and Chinese make tarts, although they are made with different pastries, short and flaky. Somehow the latter kind seems best if you serve them warm, which we think is the only way to have this pudding. You can serve this tart with a number of accompaniments. It is delicious as the centrepiece of a citrus salad, with a selection of citrus fruits or a citrus sorbet.

This dish is a single tart but you can, like the Chinese, make a separate small tart for each serving.

SERVES 8–10 OR MAKES 1 CAKE

THE TARTS

300 g (11 oz) puff pastry

8 eggs

275 ml (10 fl oz) lemon juice

275 g (10 oz) sugar

275 ml (10 fl oz) double cream

Roll out the pastry and line a 25 cm (10 in) flan ring. Cover it with foil and fill with rice, then bake in an oven preheated to 180°C (350°F) for 50 minutes or until firm.

Meanwhile, gently whisk the eggs, lemon juice and sugar, and pour onto the cream. It is important not to aerate this mixture, so whisk it gently just until completely liquid—and with no bubbles. Strain to remove any bubbles or fragments of lemon pulp.

Pour the mixture into the hot pastry case and bake at 150°C (300°F) for about 60 minutes or until the mixture has set.

FROZEN PISTACHIO NOUGATS WITH HONEY FIGS AND BISCOTTI

This is a perfect summer pudding. It is the same consistency as ice cream, but it is not at its best if you leave it in the freezer for more than a couple of days. On an average summer day, let it sit for 10 minutes before serving. Of course if the temperature outside is 40°C (88°F), then this will be a much shorter process.

Two things for this dish need to be made in advance, the praline and the custard.

SERVES 8

CUSTARD

4 tablespoons sugar

3 egg yolks

200 ml (7 fl oz) cream

1 vanilla bean, split

To make the custard, follow the method for the Cinnamon Ice Cream on page 137 until the freezing and churning stage, and omitting the cinnamon sticks.

THE PRALINE

375 g (13 oz) sugar

75 g (3 oz) hazelnuts, slowly toasted

75 g (3 oz) almonds, blanched and slowly toasted

Add 4 tablespoons of water to the sugar and cook until it just reaches a caramel, then add the hot nuts and stir them in thoroughly. Tip the mixture out onto an oiled tray or silicon paper and spread them out with an oiled wooden spoon to cool. Once the praline has cooled to solid, break it up with a rolling pin or in a food processor, and store it in an airtight jar immediately.

THE FIGS

450 g (16 oz) figs

200 ml (7 fl oz) brandy

200 ml (7 fl oz) red wine

200 ml (7 fl oz) honey

zest and juice of 1 orange

zest and juice of 1 lemon

2 cloves

2 cinnamon sticks

Soak the figs overnight in the brandy.

Next day, cover with the remaining ingredients and bring to the boil. Simmer for 20 minutes, then let them cool in the liquid. Chill in the refrigerator until ready to serve.

THE SYRUP
125 g (4 oz) sugar
60 ml (2½ fl oz) honey

1 tablespoon liquid glucose
100 ml (3½ fl oz) water

Mix all the ingredients together and bring to a soft rolling boil.

THE FROZEN NOUGAT
6 egg whites
200 ml (7 fl oz) double cream

100 g (4 oz) praline
100 g (4 oz) ground pistachio nuts
zest and juice of 1 lemon

Whisk the egg whites until they are stiff. Keep whisking and pour in the hot syrup in a steady stream. Beat for 15 minutes or until it is completely cool. Add the 250 ml (9 fl oz) custard, then the double cream and fold roughly together. Fold in the praline, the pistachio nuts, and the lemon zest and juice. Pour into moulds and freeze.

BISCOTTI Makes approximately 20 biscuits
150 g (5 oz) caster sugar
150 g (5 oz) plain flour, sifted
80 g (3 oz) pistachio nuts, unsalted

½ teaspoon baking powder
2 whole eggs
1 beaten egg, for egg wash

Combine all the ingredients except the beaten egg, adding the whole eggs last, and form a workable biscuit pastry. Roll into sausages the length of a baking sheet and 4 cm (1½ in) in diameter.

Brush with the egg wash and bake in an oven preheated to 180°C (350°F) for approximately 25 minutes or until golden. Remove from the oven and cool for 2 minutes. Slice on an angle into 1 cm (¼ in) thick slices.

Lay the biscotti on a baking sheet and return to the oven to dry out for a further 10 minutes. Cool and store in an airtight container. These can be served as petits fours, or with ice cream or sorbets, and in this case with the nougats.

To serve, unmould the nougats and serve a pile of figs beside each of them.

CARAMELISED APPLE TART AND CINNAMON ICE CREAM

Cinnamon and cloves are traditionally the spices that suit apples best. In this dish the fuller flavour of the cinnamon perfectly complements the slightly bitter taste of the caramel.

The basic ice cream custard in the recipe is one the French call Creme Anglaise (or custard), a rare enough acknowledgement of an Anglo-Saxon origin in gallic cuisine! Creme Anglaise can be served as a sauce on its own with a number of puddings—fruit tarts, poached fruits and, in a very indulgent form, as a sauce on ice cream. It is also used as a filling for pastries.

The smoothness of the custard depends on how well the egg yolks combine with milk; there is a limit to how much one will meld with the other. The closer that limit is approached, the thicker the custard will be. Some recipes add a little cream to enhance the texture once the custard has cooled. For a rich buttery ice cream, like the one in this dish, we use cream alone. To make the ice cream you will need a small domestic ice cream churn.

SERVES 8–10 OR MAKES 1 CAKE

THE APPLE TART
300 g (11 oz) puff pastry
6–8 cooking apples (Golden Delicious)
500 g (18 oz) sugar
150 ml (5 fl oz) double cream
5 eggs
a pinch of ground cinnamon

Roll out the puff pastry and line a 25 cm (10 in) flan ring, then cover the pastry with foil and fill with rice. Bake in an oven preheated to 180°C (350°F) for 50 minutes or until firm.

Meanwhile, peel, core and slice each apple into 16 pieces. Melt the sugar, without water, fairly quickly in a heavy-based pan and cook to a caramel, stirring out any lumps. Add the apples and cook until they are just soft. Strain, set the apples aside, and let cool slightly. Add the cream, eggs and cinnamon to the caramel mix. Put the apples into the pastry case and pour over the mixture, then bake for about 40 minutes at 150°C (300°F).

THE ICE CREAM
200 g (8 oz) sugar
6 egg yolks
1 L (1²/₃ pts) cream
1 vanilla bean, split
8 cinnamon sticks

To make the ice cream, whisk the sugar and egg yolks together until whitish in colour. Bring the cream, vanilla and cinnamon sticks just to the boil, then let cool just a little. Stir this mix into the whisked yolks and sugar. Replace in a clean pot and cook gently until the mixture is thick enough to easily and evenly coat the back of a wooden spoon. Again let it cool slightly and strain out the cinnamon sticks and vanilla pod. Blend the cinnamon sticks with a little of the custard, then squeeze enough of this puree to your taste through a muslin cloth into the rest of the creme. Cool the mixture in the refrigerator and churn.

WALNUT CAKE WITH MASCARPONE

The triple-cream fresh cheese used in this cake, mascarpone, is the basis of a famous Italian pudding called Tiramisu or "pick-me-up". Liberally laced with brandy, which may or may not explain the name, Tiramisu was the invention of a restaurateur in Treviso. Although a recent compilation, it is frequently presented as a traditional Italian pudding, which, in the course of time, it is bound to become.

The dish is so simple that we have included its method here. Soak fingers of sponge cake in strong espresso coffee, layer them into mascarpone that is liberally spiked with brandy and has egg yolks beaten into it, and top with dry powdered chocolate. Serve this with marc, a calvados or a fine Languedoc and be thoroughly self-indulgent, not, of course, to the point where you will need another pick-me-up.

SERVES 8 OR MAKES 1 CAKE

THE CAKE
8 eggs, separated
250 g (9 oz) icing sugar
1 tablespoon butter, for greasing
50 g (2 oz) breadcrumbs
50 g (2 oz) plain flour
250 g (9 oz) walnuts, chopped
juice and zest of 1 lemon

Whisk the yolks and half the icing sugar until they are white. Whisk the whites with the remaining sugar. Butter two 20 cm (8 in) cake tins and sprinkle with the breadcrumbs. Fold the two egg mixtures, the flour, walnuts, juice and zest together. Scrape into the two tins and bake in an oven preheated to 180°C (350°F) for 45–50 minutes. Cool, then cut each cake through the centre.

THE FILLING
250 g (9 oz) mascarpone
75 ml (3 fl oz) Dark Caramel (see page 133)
1 teaspoon coffee essence
50 ml (2 fl oz) brandy
16 walnut halves, to decorate

Mix all the ingredients into an easily spreading cream—you may or may not need to use a little extra caramel to achieve this. Place one cake layer in the bottom of an 18 cm (7 in) deep cake tin and spread over a generous layer of filling. Continue until all layers have been used. Place the fourth cake layer on top and weight with a plate or cake board. Remove the ring and finish spreading the sides and top with the remaining mascarpone mixture. Decorate with walnuts and serve with custard.

CHAMPAGNE AND GRAPEFRUIT GRANITA WITH STONE FRUITS

This, apart from the attention it needs in the freezer, is a very simple and elegant dish. It is not a sorbet, but is full of ice crystals—more like one of those shaved ice drinks, covered with cordial, that are served at the Easter Show. Serve it either alone or with fresh, chilled or poached peaches, nectarines or cherries.

SERVES 6–8

THE SYRUP

260 g (9½ oz) sugar
200 ml (7 fl oz) water

Make the sugar syrup by bringing the sugar and water to a rolling boil. Stop the sugar from crystallising by brushing the sides of the pan with cold water. Cool, then chill until required. Any unused syrup can be stored for poaching fruit or for making fruit jelly, such as the dish on page 145.

THE GRANITA

300 ml (11 fl oz) champagne
900 ml (1²/₃ pts) grapefruit juice

Mix all ingredients with 300 ml (11 fl oz) sugar syrup and freeze, stirring every hour until frozen.

How many puddings are as easy as this?

THE FRUIT
6–8 freestone peaches

6–8 small nectarines
6–8 apricots

Poach the fruit in the remaining syrup for 5 minutes. They should still be a bit firm inside. Stone the fruit and serve in a dish, with a pile of frozen granita alongside.

BUTTERMILK BAVAROIS

The bavarois should never be confused with bavaroise, which is not a pudding but a cold drink made from alcohol, milk and tea. Both come from Bavaria and the first is another version of a milk, cream and egg yolk custard— very rich, and for very thin, well exercised people who eat it only once in a while. For the rest of us, in its original rich form it ought to be a very occasional delight.

We make this version with buttermilk, which gives it a slightly sour and refreshing flavour and, although still made with cream, does not carry quite the same health warning. Unlike the original this does not use eggs.

SERVES 8

1 L (1²/₃ pts) cream
1 vanilla bean, split
150 g (5 oz) sugar

5 sheets of gelatine,
softened in a little cold water
300 ml (11 fl oz) cream
1 L (1²/₃ pts) buttermilk

Heat the 1 L of cream with the vanilla bean and sugar until the sugar has dissolved, then add the gelatine. Let the mixture cool slowly.

Half whip the 300 ml (11 fl oz) cream. Add the buttermilk to the cooled cream and sugar mixture and remove the vanilla bean. When the buttermilk mixture is on the point of setting, gently fold in the half-whipped cream and pour into 8 x 200 ml (7 fl oz) dariole moulds. Chill until set, and serve with berries or passionfruit.

Orange Almond Cake with Orange Junket   See page 144

Amaretto Parfait with Muscatelles and Almond Tuilles   See page 143

AMARETTO PARFAIT WITH MUSCATELLES AND ALMOND TUILLES

A maretto has a slightly romantic legend attached to it. Bernadino Luini, the sixteenth century Italian painter, used the beautiful wife of an inn keeper as a model for the Madonna. The woman, flattered by the distinction, gave him a jug of aquavite that had been marinated with ground almond kernels. Personally, I think, he would have been better off drinking the aquavite in its original form, as Amaretto, to our palette, is best used for cooking.

SERVES 8 OR MAKES 1 CAKE

THE MUSCATELLES

8 small bunches muscatelles

750 ml (1¼ pts) red wine

10 peppercorns

Choose muscatelles that still have their stalks. Bring them to the boil in the red wine and peppercorns, and simmer for 20 minutes. Chill in the liquid overnight.

THE PARFAIT

10 egg yolks

250 g (9 oz) sugar

125 ml (4 fl oz) Amaretto

1 litre (1²/₃ pts) double cream

1 Almond Base (see page 133)

Whisk the yolks and the sugar until white, then add the Amaretto. Lightly whip the cream and fold into the mix. Pour into a 20 cm (8 in) ring, lined with the almond base and sitting on a 23 cm (9 in) cake board. Freeze.

To serve, sit the parfait on the bench for 5 minutes. Remove the ring and serve with a bunch of muscatelles.

MAKES 12

ALMOND TUILLES

150 g (5 oz) almonds

150 g (5 oz) sugar

25 g (1 oz) flour

4 egg whites

3 tablespoons melted butter

Mix all ingredients together, adding the melted butter last. Refrigerate the mixture overnight.

Spoon the mixture onto hot, greased, black steel trays and bake in an oven preheated to 150°C (300°F) for approximately 10–15 minutes or until brown and dried out. Scrape from the trays and shape over a rolling pin while hot. Seal in an airtight tin.

ORANGE ALMOND CAKE WITH ORANGE JUNKET

This delicious nutty cake has its origins in the Middle East. It can be served with a simple salad of orange segments served in their juice. The cool, slippery and fragrant junket in this recipe is a splendid foil to the texture of the cake.

Junket can be flavoured with many scents, most usually flower waters or with the rose geranium petals that Stephanie Alexander prefers. Junket is best when it *is* junket—that chilly, shimmering stuff that grandmothers used to make—and not some bewildered cross between double cream and custard. Our grandmothers, of course, would not have made their junkets any other colour than white, and certainly not flavoured them with geranium, or any other flower. It is time to rescue this often despised dish from its English nursery past and restore it to a more exotic role where it equally belongs.

SERVES 12

THE CAKE

3 oranges

9 fresh eggs

375 g (13 oz) sugar

375 g (13 oz) almond meal

2 teaspoons baking powder

Simmer the whole oranges for 2 hours, changing the water three times. Let them cool, then halve, remove any seeds, and squeeze out any liquid absorbed during cooking. Whisk the eggs and sugar for a couple of minutes, then add the oranges and puree in a blender. Mix in the almonds and baking powder, pour into a 30 cm (12 in) greased and lined cake tin and bake in an oven preheated to 180°C (350°F) for 40–50 minutes.

THE JUNKET

zest of 1 orange

100 g (4 oz) sugar

2 squirts of orange flower water

1 L (1²/₃ pts) milk

4 crushed junket tablets, dissolved in a little water

Mix the zest, sugar and orange flower water and macerate for 15 minutes. Warm the milk to blood heat, 37°C (98°F), and add the mixture. Stir in the dissolved junket tablets last and pour into ramekins. Let stand for 30 minutes at room temperature, then refrigerate.

THIN PEAR TARTS

T his is such a simple pudding that given a pear or two and some puff pastry you might have invented it yourself. Simple or not, it makes a fine pudding served with a vanilla ice cream.

Make the ice cream as for the Caramelised Apple Tart (see page 137), just leaving out the cinnamon.

MAKES 6 SMALL TARTS

THE PEAR TART
700 g (1½ lb) puff pastry
4–6 large pears, peeled, cored and thinly sliced

100 g (4 oz) caster sugar
50 g (2 oz) butter
icing sugar, for dusting

Roll the pastry out into a sheet 20 cm (8 in) wide by 40 cm (16 in) long. Cut into 20 cm (8 in) rounds with a cake tin. Cover with the paper-thin slices of pear, sprinkle with sugar and small nuts of butter, and bake in an oven preheated to 180°C (350°F) for 40 minutes. Dust the cooked tart with icing sugar and serve warm with the ice cream.

FRUIT JELLY AND FRIED PASTRIES WITH MANGO

T his simple fruit jelly can be made from any fruit pulp you fancy. We use passionfruit for its strong, unambiguous flavour. It also pairs well with the mango and the slightly sour taste of buttermilk.

SERVES 8

THE JELLY
800 ml (1½ pts) passionfruit pulp
11 sheets of gelatine (10 teaspoons powdered gelatine)

400 ml (14 fl oz) Sugar Syrup (see page 139)
lime or lemon juice, to taste

Push the passionfruit pulp through a fine strainer. Soak the gelatine in a little cold water to soften. Bring one third of the sugar syrup and fruit mixture to a gentle boil. Dissolve the gelatine in the remaining hot sugar syrup, then stir it in to the remaining syrup and fruit pulp mix, adding the lime or lemon juice to taste. Let the mixture cool and just at the point where it is beginning to set, pour it into 8 dariole moulds and refrigerate. The jellies will take about 2 hours to set properly. They do not keep, so serve them the same day.

THE FRIED PASTRIES
2 L (3½ pts) grape seed oil, for frying
500 g (18 oz) puff pastry
icing sugar, to dust

4 mangoes, peeled
500 ml (18 fl oz) buttermilk
100 ml (3½ fl oz) cream

Heat the oil in a deep-fryer to 180°C (350°F).

Roll the pastry out into a long rectangle about 20 cm (8 in) wide and 3 mm (⅛ in) thick. Cut it into 16 strips. Fold or twist these into different shapes. We slice down the centre of each strip, keeping both ends intact, and fold one end through the middle, giving it a twist something like a pretzel or bow tie. In North Africa these pastries sometimes have sesame seeds pressed into them.

Fry them in small numbers to keep the oil at a constant heat, allowing 3–4 minutes to brown each side. Drain the pastries on absorbent paper and sieve a generous dusting of icing sugar over while they are still hot.

Serve the pastries and turned-out jellies with two peeled mango quarters each, and with the combined buttermilk and cream poured over.

Supper

In England, Edwardian gentlemen knew that the quickest way to an actress's heart was through her supper. The meal has had a slightly rakish tilt to it ever since. Those British bucks were following in a long tradition and the idea of an intimate meal for two served late in the evening, and preceding an amorous encounter, has been around for a very long time. It is, of course, attributed to the French and according to Larousse, French roués in the eighteenth century used to help the hotel chefs of Paris prepare the meal.

Naturally enough, a lot of favourite dishes for these suppers were fashioned from those ingredients thought to have aphrodisiacal properties—oysters and asparagus for example—and they were always to be washed down with copious amounts of champagne. Suppers on a larger and less intimate scale, like those held at the conclusion of a ball, sported grander dishes of game birds, venison and wild boar, and great varieties of nourishing soups.

Soups are still a preferred supper dish, intimate or not, and we suggest some in this chapter. They have the advantage of being easily prepared in advance and can perfectly reflect the weather—chilled, crisp-flavoured soups on steamy summer nights, and robust, substantial broths for the more savage winter environment.

In ordinary life, supper has much more prosaic origins than its form in Edwardian London or eighteenth century Paris, and in its original form was simply the evening meal—now called dinner. Where dinners are still eaten at midday, the terms supper and tea are interchangeable for the light, final meal of the day.

If you are preparing food to be eaten late at night, then keep it light, nourishing and simple. Most supper components can be prepared in advance and we suggest some interesting butters and salads. If you do wish to fix a salad well beforehand, wash, carefully dry the leaves and store them in a covered container in the refrigerator to crisp. In a sort of garden version of a marinade, you can lay the leaves on top of some sprigs of strong herbs, like fresh basil or rosemary, and you will be surprised how much of their flavours the salad leaves take up.

Since supper should be simple, it demands invention and innovation. Small dishes and memorable flavours ought to be the benchmark for this very interesting meal.

SPICY LAMB SOUP WITH CHICK PEAS

S picy soups are a staple lunch or supper dish in the Middle East. Some of those aromatic wonders, thick with cereals and chunks of meat, just hover on the edge of being stews. Soup is a dish that can be eaten all hours and as the French know, a savoury soup is a splendid way to begin or end a day.

This soup is served with a garnish made from toasted spices sharpened with vinegar and chopped Italian parsley and coriander. The dish is finished with yoghurt thinned with cream.

SERVES 8

THE SOUP

100 g (4 oz) chickpeas, soaked overnight
salt and pepper, to taste
400 g (14 oz) lamb shoulder, chopped
2½ teaspoons cumin
2½ teaspoons coriander seeds
100 g (4 oz) spicy dry sausage
100 g (4 oz) chicken giblets, cleaned
olive oil

2 teaspoons black mustard seeds
2 teaspoons paprika
1 medium potato, peeled
1 medium onion, shredded
1 medium carrot, shredded
1 medium turnip, shredded
1.1 L (2 pts) Veal Stock (see page 22)
4 tablespoons raisins

Drain the chickpeas and cover with fresh cold water. Do not season. Bring the water to the boil and simmer the chickpeas, skimming off the froth, until they are soft. This will take about 1 hour. About 10 minutes before the end of cooking, season with salt and pepper. Set the cooked peas aside in their liquid.

Cover the lamb meat with cold water and bring to the boil to remove any dirt or excess fat from the meat. Discard the liquid. Grind and toast the cumin and coriander seeds and set half a teaspoon of each aside for the garnish. Slice the sausage and fry it with the chicken giblets and lamb meat in the olive oil until they are golden brown. Add the ground spices, the mustard seeds and paprika, and fry for a couple of minutes more.

Cover all the vegetables with the stock, then add the meat mixture and raisins. Bring to the boil and simmer for 40 minutes, skimming off the fat regularly. Drain the chickpeas and add them to the soup and simmer for another 15 minutes. Check the seasoning.

THE GARNISH

1 red Spanish onion, peeled
2 tablespoons balsamic vinegar
½ teaspoon ground black pepper
½ teaspoon saffron powder

½ bunch coriander leaves, coarsely chopped
½ bunch Italian parsley leaves, coarsely chopped
100 ml (3½ fl oz) yoghurt, preferably made from sheep's milk
4 tablespoons cream

Chop the onion and marinate it in the vinegar for 15 minutes. Tip out the excess vinegar and mix in the pepper, saffron, coriander and parsley, as well as the reserved spice from the soup. Thin the yoghurt with a little cream until it has a runny consistency.

Serve the soup in a large bowl with the yoghurt-cream mix drizzled over the top and sprinkled with the garnish.

CHILLED SNAPPER SOUP WITH PASTINA

This deliciously thick soup should be well chilled before it is served. It is a rich yellow colour, the result of the hot stock being whisked into the eggs in the same way that the Greek lemon sauce, Avgolemono, is made. The pastina used in this dish is almost always served in stock or soup.

SERVES 4–6

THE SNAPPER SOUP
1 kg (2 lb 3 oz) whole snapper
1 medium onion, sliced
1 large leek, sliced
½ bunch parsley stalks, chopped

juice of 1 orange
juice of 2 lemons
1 bay leaf
cracked white pepper, to taste
1.5 L (2½ pts) Fish Stock (see page 23)

Trim off the head, gut and scale the fish and rinse under a cold tap. Put the fish with all the other ingredients in a pot and cover with the fish stock. Bring to the boil and poach for 20 minutes. Let the fish cool in the liquid.

THE PASTINA
100 g (4 oz) pastina

4 eggs
½ bunch red basil leaves

Boil the pastina in a pot of lightly salted boiling water until al dente. This will only take a couple of minutes. Refresh under cold water and drain.

Take the cooked snapper out of the poaching liquid, skin and bone it and flake the flesh. Set the flesh aside. Strain the fish stock into a clean pot and bring it back to the boil. You should have 1.5 L (2½ pts).

Whisk the eggs in a bowl until light and fluffy, then gradually add the hot stock, whisking vigorously. Transfer the egg and stock mixture to a clean pot and cook gently, stirring all the while, until it thickens. Do not boil.

Chill the eggs and stock mix. Add the snapper flesh and fold in the pastina. Chill well and serve with a sprinkling of red basil leaves.

DUCK AND WATERCRESS SOUP WITH GLUTEN DUMPLINGS

Gluten flour is used primarily in China and Japan as a versatile source of protein. It is a good vegetarian basic. It can be cooked in a variety of ways, braised with vegetables, fried in batter, served in a miso sauce or in soup as dumplings—which we do in this dish.

Gluten is the component of wheat flour that makes it suitable for bread as the gluten molecules can change shape under pressure and then revert back to their original shape. This way they trap and disperse gases from yeast through the bread dough without breaking, or building up large pockets of gas surrounded by heavy, dense bread.

Making the gluten dough is a lengthy process, but the result is worth it and the dough freezes well.

SERVES 8

THE DUMPLINGS
250 ml (9 oz) gluten flour
125 g (4 oz) plain flour

300 ml (11 fl oz) water
50 ml (2 fl oz) Caramel (see page 133)

Place all the ingredients in a mixing bowl and form a dough. Knead thoroughly for 15 minutes, then set aside for 1 hour in a bowl covered with water. Drain off the water, pour on more fresh water and knead the dough under the water, changing the water each time it becomes cloudy. When the water finally remains clear, all the starch has been extracted from the dough and you are left with the gluten. Store the dough in the water in the refrigerator or freezer for several weeks or until you need it.

THE DUCK SOUP
3 medium carrots, peeled and diced
3 small onions, peeled and diced
6 sticks celery, peeled and diced
4 large ripe tomatoes, whole

1 x No. 19—1.8 kg (4 lb) duckling, washed
2 L (3½ pts) Chicken or Duck Stock (see page 23)
4 tablespoons thin soy sauce
½ bunch watercress

Divide the vegetables into two. Make a bed of half the vegetables and tomatoes in a roasting pan and roast the duck on them in an oven preheated to 200°C (400°F) until it is dark brown.

Take the duck and the vegetables out of the dish, being careful not to lift any fat with them, and put them in a pot with the rest of the vegetables and cover with some of the stock.

Pour the fat out of the roasting dish and deglaze the dish with the remaining stock. Add the cooking juices to the soup and cook this for 1½ hours. Lift the duck out of the liquid and put it aside until cool enough to handle, then skin and shred it. Strain the soup into a clean pot and bring it back to the boil. Simmer gently and check the seasoning.

Cut the gluten dough into strips and marinate it in the thin soy sauce. Braise these strips for 15 minutes in some of the soup.

Skim any fat from the soup and add the watercress leaves. Chop the watercress stalks and throw those in too. The cress, leaves and stalks should be added at the last moment and should remain a vivid green.

Serve the soup in deep bowls with the shredded meat and floating dumplings.

CRAB CONSOMME WITH TAMARIND CUSTARD

There is nothing rustic or countrified about a consomme. They are the most refined branch of the soup family and can be usefully employed for a clam supper dish with pretensions to elegance.

To emphasise that point, we offer this dish with a royal garnish, in this instance flavoured with tamarind and ginger rather than egg, tomato or spinach.

SERVES 8

THE CUSTARD

75 g (3 oz) tamarind

zest of 2 limes

2 tablespoons grated ginger root

500 ml (18 fl oz) Fish Stock (see page 23)

4 eggs

8 egg yolks

1 tablespoon butter, for greasing

In a pot, mix the tamarind, lime zest, ginger and stock. Bring to the boil and simmer for 5 minutes. Strain the mix and let it cool. Beat together the whole eggs and the yolks, and whisk them into the cooled stock.

Strain this mixture into a shallow, buttered cake tin. Place it in a dish filled with water and bake in an oven preheated to 140°C (275°F) for 1 hour. Let the custard cool.

THE CRAB

6 medium-sized blue swimmer crabs

50 ml (2 fl oz) olive oil

2 cloves garlic, crushed

3 L (5½ pts) Fish Stock (see page 23)

Thoroughly crush and smash the crabs with a cleaver. Heat the oil in a deep ovenproof pan, large enough to hold the stock. Fry the crabs and garlic, then roast them for 10 minutes in an oven preheated to 200°C (400°F).

In another pan, bring the stock to the boil, pour it over the crabs, then let it return to the boil and simmer for 30 minutes. Strain the stock, and as much crab meat as possible, through a conical strainer and let cool.

THE CONSOMME CLARIFICATION

4 medium tomatoes

2 medium onions

1 large leek, green removed

1 small hot chilli, seeded

8 large sprigs of Vietnamese mint, chopped

7 egg whites

Puree the tomatoes, onions and leek in a blender. Transfer to a large clean pot. Whisk the chilli, mint and egg whites through the puree. Whisk the cooled crab stock in to this.

Put the mixture back on to heat and bring it to the boil, stirring all the time until the mixture appears to be setting and looks white around the edges. Reduce the heat to low, then gradually bring it back to simmer for 45 minutes, until the top has set and the stock has had time to clarify through a "raft" of solid ingredients.

Remove from the heat, carefully make a hole in the raft and gently ladle the soup out and through a strainer, lined with a clean wet tea towel or muslin cloth, into a clean pot. Return this to the heat and bring back to a gentle, soft boil.

Cut the custard into large cubes and put them in the bottom of the soup bowls. Pour the consomme over the top and serve.

SOFT-BOILED EGGS AND ASPARAGUS SALAD WITH CALABRESE SAUSAGE

Chilli is one of the favourite spices of Calabria, the region of Italy that forms the toe of the boot, and the Calabrese sausage in this dish is a dried salami liberally flavoured with it. It makes a pleasantly assertive foil to the blandness of the eggs and the bocconcini.

Asparagus is one of those traditional supper dishes that was once believed to provoke more than one kind of appetite. Perhaps the undoubtedly phallic shape of the vegetable had something to do with that notion—certainly nothing else about it has been established as an active ingredient in the amorous repertoire!

Asparagus deserves to be superbly cooked, not limp at the head and woody at the cut ends.

SERVES 4–6

THE SALAD

4 bundles asparagus

8–12 fresh eggs

4 tablespoons butter

4–6 x 50 g (2 oz) bocconcini, sliced thinly

175 g (6 oz) good Calabrese sausage

fresh ground sea salt and black pepper, to taste

Cook the asparagus spears to perfection. There are a number of schools of thought about how these should be prepared. Some insist that they are completely peeled to where the flowering tip begins. Others suggest that they only need to be broken at the base. And some aesthetes like to sharpen the base so the yellow contrasts against the dark green of the stem. Make your own decisions with this.

Boil the eggs for 4½–5 minutes so the yolks are still bright yellow and runny and the whites are set. Cool under cold running water until the eggs have cooled enough to shell.

Melt the butter slowly so it does not separate or begin to cook. Arrange a pile of hot asparagus in the centre of each plate and dress with the melted butter. Scatter the slices of bocconcini and sausage over the piles and place two eggs on top of each. Cut one of the eggs open to display the bright yellow yolk. Season the entire dish with salt and pepper.

GLAZED KASSLER CHOPS AND GINGER PUDDING WITH SCRAMBLED EGGS

The charcuterie and delicatessen are natural allies of the brasserie cook. Their products, often prepared in quite complex ways, give the domestic cook, who aspires to make simple but savoury dishes, more than a head start.

Pork kassler is typical. Strictly speaking kassler is the cured and smoked eye of the pork loin, but in Australia and New Zealand the description often includes the whole loin still on the bone. In Switzerland these smoked pork chops are called *rippli* and are often served as a picnic dish.

The ginger puddings in this supper are an aromatic version of the Yorkshire pudding, but they are perhaps a little healthier, not being cooked in meat dripping but in their own steam.

These puddings are dead easy to make. You can prepare them well in advance and, if you like, leave them in the cold oven and simply turn it on to cook from scratch when you get home. If the puddings are cooked enough, they will easily hold for up to half an hour before eating, but then they will slump and look more than a little forlorn, although they are still delicious. They will also collapse if you sit them in a draught or open the oven while they are cooking.

In theory scrambled eggs are fashioned after the same principle as omelettes and they require the same developed and tender skills to cook them to perfection. One difference though is that the scrambled eggs hold a little more liquid than the omelette mix and cook at a lower and slower heat.

SERVES 6

THE GINGER PUDDINGS

2 tablespoons butter, for greasing ramekins

2 tablespoons soft breadcrumbs

pinch or two of sea salt

1 knob 4 cm (1½ in) ginger root, grated

350 ml (12 fl oz) milk

150 g (5 oz) plain flour

2 large eggs

pinch of salt

Thoroughly butter six 200 ml (7 fl oz) ramekins and sprinkle them with the breadcrumbs and sea salt. Put a generous pinch of the grated ginger in each.

Put milk, flour, eggs and salt into a blender and mix until the consistency of pouring cream. Do not overmix. Pour the mixture into ramekins and bake the puddings in an oven preheated to 220°C (425°F) for 30–35 minutes or until they are dark brown and well risen. Be careful not to open the oven during cooking and if they begin to go too dark, reduce the heat by 25°C (75°F) or so.

THE KASSLER CHOPS

3 tablespoons grated fresh ginger root

125 ml (4 fl oz) dark honey

175 ml (6 fl oz) apple cider

½ tablespoon freshly ground black pepper

zest of 3 lemons

6 x 100 g (4 oz) kassler chops with bone

½ bunch chopped parsley

Mix all the ingredients together, reserving the chopped parsley for the garnish, and marinate the chops in a roasting dish. Make sure they are well basted and sprinkled with black pepper just before they go into the oven. Bake at 220°C (425°F) for 10 minutes or until golden brown.

THE SCRAMBLED EGGS

12 eggs

100 ml (3½ fl oz) cream

100 g (4 oz) Chilli Butter (see page 27)

½ bunch chopped parsley

Lightly whisk the eggs together. Bring the cream quickly to the boil in a stainless steel pot, reduce the heat and mix in the eggs, stirring continuously as they cook. Just before they set, whisk in the chilli butter and remove them from the heat. The egg and butter mix should still be quite moist.

Cut open the puddings with a sharp knife and spoon a generous dollop of the scrambled egg into each. Serve each chop with a pudding and some of the remaining egg, then garnish the chops with some of their glaze and a scattering of the chopped parsley.

SPINACH SALAD, CRISPY BACON, PINE NUTS AND SOFT-BOILED EGGS

The combination of eggs and spinach is reasonably classic. They turn up in old-fashioned Oeufs Florentine—poached eggs served on spinach and tossed with butter and Parmesan—and in spinach omelettes, of which there are at least five traditional varieties. Somehow the two ingredients seem to make a perfect marriage of texture, flavour and colour.

For this dish choose the smallest spinach leaves you can find. They are by far the sweetest.

At the Brasserie a variation of this dish is served with sieved hard-boiled eggs, but here we suggest cooking and serving the eggs the same way as for Soft-Boiled Eggs and Asparagus Salad with Calabrese Sausage, on page 153.

SERVES 4–6

THE SALAD

8–12 bacon rashers (very thin)

8–12 eggs

8–12 slices of stale French bread

1 large clove garlic, halved

175 ml (6 fl oz) olive oil

1 teaspoon Dijon mustard

4 tablespoons white wine vinegar

sea salt and pepper, to taste

3–4 bunches spinach leaves, washed and dried

4 tablespoons pine nuts, toasted

Bring the rashers of bacon to the boil in cold water, drain and cut into strips. Boil the eggs. Rub the bread slices with the garlic. Dry the flavoured bread in a 180°C (350°F) oven until crunchy.

Heat 2 tablespoons of the oil in a pan and toss the bacon in it until crisp and brown. Whisk the remaining oil into the mustard and vinegar. Season with salt and pepper. Toss the spinach leaves in a bowl with the vinaigrette.

To serve, arrange the leaves on the plates and sprinkle them with the pine nuts and crispy bacon. Tuck the bread slices in the side and top the spinach with the eggs, cutting one of them open. Season the whole dish with sea salt and black pepper.

BRIOCHE WITH CHICKEN LIVERS AND A WITLOOF AND NUT SALAD

For this dish use half the Brioche recipe on page 32. When you have made the dough mixture, quickly roll it into a French loaf shape and let it prove in a long French loaf mould. Bake the loaf in an oven preheated to 200°C (400°F) until a golden brown. This loaf shape will take about 40 minutes to cook.

Cut the finished loaf into 6 cm (2½ in) segments, one for each serve, and scoop out the centres leaving a base on each. You can store these prepared segments in the refrigerator or freezer until you toast them in the oven just before serving.

SERVES 4–6

THE CHICKEN LIVERS

400 g (14 oz) chicken livers
a few drops hazelnut oil
3 tablespoons olive oil
2 tablespoons unsalted butter
6 spring onions, chopped

flour, for dredging
100 g (4 oz) smoked bacon
200 ml (7 fl oz) Chicken Stock (see page 23)
a sprig of thyme
125 g (4 oz) Spinach Butter, cold and chopped (see page 28)

Carefully clean the livers, removing any green parts, and separate them into their natural segments. Sprinkle with a few drops of the hazelnut oil and set aside. Toast the brioche pieces either under a grill or in an oven preheated to 200°C (400°F) until golden brown.

Heat the olive oil in a pan and add the unsalted butter. Saute the chopped onions. Lightly dredge the livers in flour and cook them, with the onions, for 1 minute on each side. Remove from the pan and add the bacon to colour lightly. Mix the bacon and livers together in a bowl and drain well. Discard the oil and butter from the pan and deglaze it with the chicken stock, and add a sprig of thyme. Reduce the stock by half and whisk the spinach butter through it.

THE SALAD

4 tablespoons olive oil
1 tablespoon hazelnut oil
2 tablespoons raspberry vinegar

salt and pepper, to taste
4 shoots witloof, separated and washed
100 g (4 oz) hazelnuts, toasted

Whisk the olive and hazelnut oils into the vinegar, then season with salt and pepper. Toss the leaves and nuts in the vinaigrette.

To serve, combine the liver and bacon, spinach and butter, and spoon into the toasted brioche. Serve with the salad on the side.

OYSTER TARTLETS WITH MUSHROOM BUTTER

No supper cook could consider themselves well armed without at least one oyster dish in their repertoire. There is attached to this succulent shellfish such a body of amorous legend that faint-hearted Edwardian actresses (if there were any such things) must have immediately swooned at the sight of a dish of them, while their gentlemen beaus leered and twirled their moustachios.

Sadly, perhaps, there is not the slightest evidence to support the oyster's reputation, notwithstanding reports that Casanova ate fifty of them, with his punch, of an evening.

Whatever else the oyster might stimulate, there is no doubt that for several thousand years, it has captured the hearts of gourmets in every culture that has encountered it from the ancient Romans on. There are only a few edible species, but because the fish takes on the characteristics of its environment, rather than its parentage, the merits of this or that oyster are hotly debated. To southern New Zealanders, for instance, there is no oyster in the world to compare with the deep-dredged Bluff oyster from Fouveaux Strait, while Australians swear by the Jervis Bay variety and New South Welshmen by their own Sydney rock oyster (while they might actually be consuming the same creature from Victoria).

SERVES 6

THE PASTRY (enough for 8 cases)
225 g (8 oz) unsalted butter
250 g (9 oz) plain flour

½ teaspoon salt
2 eggs

This pastry can be prepared and made into tartlet cases in advance. It is quite easy to make provided a few rules are kept in mind: do not overwork the pastry, or heat the butter to the extent that it melts and becomes too soft and oily.

Cut the butter into small pieces and, if it has come straight out of the refrigerator, let them stand until at room temperature. Work the butter into the flour and salt, using only the fingertips and thumbs. When the mixture resembles breadcrumbs, add the eggs. Mix together for a few minutes but do not overmix. Cover the dough with plastic wrap and let it rest for 1 hour.

Roll the dough out as thinly as possible. Lightly butter 6 tartlet cases and line them with the dough. Prick the bottoms, cut off any excess pastry and squeeze the edges up about 1 cm (½ in). Rest the filled cases in the refrigerator for 30 minutes or so.

Preheat the oven to 180°C (350°F) and bake the cases for 15–20 minutes or until they are golden brown. Cool on a cooling rack. These finished cases can be stored in an airtight container until you are on the brink of the supper.

THE OYSTERS

400 g (14 oz) oyster mushrooms

salt and pepper, to taste

1 large bunch sorrel leaves, shredded

4 dozen oysters

125 g (4 oz) Mushroom Butter (see page 27)

Heat a steel or teflon-coated pan until hot and dry fry the mushrooms without oil or butter. Season them. Arrange the sorrel leaves in the tarlet cases and cover with the mushrooms. Top the tartlets with the raw oysters and place a slice of mushroom butter on each. Grill them for 5 minutes or until they are heated through.

EGGPLANT AND PROSCIUTTO SANDWICH

A sandwich in the acceptable order of things is assembled between slices of bread. In this dish we substitute slices of eggplant so it is really only a metaphorical sandwich. Metaphorical or not, it is a delicious supper which can be prepared in advance, just leaving the 15 minutes of oven baking as the final step before serving. You can usefully employ that time by making the salad.

Experiment, if you have a mind to, with other fillings and other cheeses than the ones we suggest here. Pitted olives are a good idea for example and so are anchovies.

The cheese we use is stracchino, since it is an excellent melting cheese, and its flavour complements that of the eggplant. If you wish, try gruyere, provolone or goat's cheese.

SERVES 6

THE SANDWICH

3 large eggplants

sea salt

12 slices prosciutto

1 red and 1 yellow capsicum, grilled
    and peeled

6 thick slices stracchino

18 dried tomatoes

3 eggs

soft breadcrumbs

olive oil

salt and pepper, to taste

Cut the eggplants into 6 flat slices, as opposed to rounds, big enough to make the sandwich halves. Put the slices in a dish and sprinkle with sea salt. Leave them for 30 minutes to degorge.

Carefully wipe the eggplant and place the prosciutto, capsicums, stracchino and tomatoes on half the slices. Put the other slices on top and press firmly to make a sandwich. Whisk the eggs together, then dip the eggplant sandwiches into the mix and thoroughly crumb them. Let them sit for a while to set.

Thin Pear Tart with Cinnamon Ice Cream   See page 145

Frozen Pistachio Nougats with Honey Figs and Biscotti   See page 135

Heat the olive oil in a pan until hot. Season the sandwiches, choosing the best side, or serving side to go down first in the pan. Cook the serving side to a golden brown, then turn and cook the other side. Transfer the sandwiches to a tray and bake in an oven preheated to 200°C (400°F) for 15 minutes. Reserve the cooking juices in the pan.

THE SALAD
3 bunches rocket leaves
extra virgin olive oil

juice of 1 lemon
2 medium tomatoes, peeled, seeded and chopped
sea salt and black pepper

Wash and carefully dry the leaves. Dress them with the oil and lemon juice, sprinkle with the chopped tomato and season with the salt and pepper.

Arrange the salad on plates and place a sandwich in the middle of each. Dress each sandwich with a little of the reserved cooking juices.

FRITTATA WITH FOUGASSE

This is a cunning combination of an Italian omelette and a French pastry to make a Spanish dish, which is really what antipodean and brasserie cooking should be all about.

The Spanish version of the omelette is called *tortilla*, and when it is served in this manner, between 2 slices of bread, it is called a *bocadillo*. It makes a fine picnic dish as well as a substantial supper. You can serve it with any kind of prepared meat you fancy—dried sausage, ham, air-dried beef, or mortadella will all do equally well.

Make half the fougasse in the method given for the Four Styles of Marinated Fish recipe on page 70.

SERVES 4
THE FRITTATA
100 ml (3½ fl oz) olive oil
1 medium potato, peeled and chopped
2 cloves garlic, chopped
4 eggs

150 g (5 oz) shelled peas
2 red capsicums
½ bunch red basil leaves
350 g (12 oz) stracchino cheese, sliced
150 g (5 oz) sausage, sliced

Heat half the olive oil in a pan and fry the potato until cooked to a crispy brown, adding the garlic about halfway through. Drain the cooked potato and garlic and wipe the pan clean. Beat the eggs lightly together and add the cooked potato and garlic, and all the other ingredients except the cheese and sausage.

Heat a little more oil in the pan and fry a quarter of the mixture, making sure some of all the ingredients are included. Fry both sides until brown and set aside in a warm place.

Cut each piece of fougasse through the middle and each frittata in half. Make a sandwich, layering the frittata, stracchino and sausage between the two pieces of fougasse, and cut in half to serve. If you have made these in advance, brush them with some olive oil and reheat in the oven.

CALF'S KIDNEY AND SAUSAGE CREPINETTES WITH BEANS AND PEPPER BUTTER

This is quite a substantial winter supper.

Crepinettes are flat cakes of meat cooked inside an envelope of pork caul, that flat veiny sheet of fat which covers the animal's innards. Those unaccustomed to offal might find this particular ingredient a little hard to handle at first, but its ability to keep its contents moist and succulent while being cooked should persuade them of its merits.

The sausage we suggest for this dish is a fresh porcellino, but any spicy sausage like chorizo, for instance, will do just as well. It should be fresh and moist, though, rather than dried.

SERVES 4–6

THE ONIONS FOR THE FILLING
3 medium-sized red Spanish onions, sliced
2 tablespoons butter
125 g (4 oz) brown sugar

a good pinch of sea salt
½ teaspoon freshly ground black pepper
2 cloves
300 ml (11 fl oz) balsamic vinegar

Saute the onions in the butter until they are tender, but without colour. Add the sugar and seasonings, deglaze with the vinegar and cook until reduced to a thick and sticky mixture.

THE MEATS AND BEANS
300 g (11 oz) fresh borlotti beans, shelled
700 g (1½ lb) calf's kidneys
100 g (4 oz) porcellino sausage
12 sheets of pig's caul 15–20 cm (6–8 in), soaked overnight

3 tablespoons olive oil
200 ml (7 fl oz) Veal Stock (see page 22)
1 recipe of Red Capsicum butter (see page 103)
red basil leaves

Cook the beans in salted water for 20–30 minutes or until tender. Refresh in cold water.

Carefully clean the kidneys and cut them into their natural segments. Seal the sausage in a very hot pan or on the barbecue, then slice it thinly. Mix the kidneys and sausage with the reduced onion mix and season.

Spread about 200 g (7 oz) of the meat and onion mix onto one piece of caul, place another sheet on top and roll carefully into a flat envelope. These should be as flat as possible, otherwise the contents will take too long to cook, leaving the outsides hard and dry.

Heat the olive oil in an ovenproof pan. Choose the best side of the envelopes as the serving side and place this side down in the pan. Brown the envelopes, then turn them over and transfer to an oven preheated to 180°C (350°F) to cook for a further 5 minutes.

Put the cooked crepinettes into a warm serving dish. Tip out the excess fat from the cooking pan and deglaze the pan with the veal stock. Heat the cooked beans in the stock and then thicken the sauce by whisking the cold, chopped red capsicum butter through it. At this point the stock should be just off the boil, no hotter.

Pour the sauce over each crepinette and sprinkle with the red basil leaves.

SEARED MACKEREL WITH SPICE NOODLES

Mackerel are oily-fleshed fish best eaten small. Available in spring and early summer, they can be soused, smoked, salted or eaten fresh. They are not good keepers so make sure that they are very fresh.

The strong flavour of the fish lends itself to joining with spice and chilli. In this dish the tasty spice noodles and vinegar sauce smell and taste wonderful with the quickly fried fillets. The noodles can be a bit of a bore to make if you are not experienced at them, but with a bit of practice this dish is quick, cheap and simple to make.

SERVES 4–6

THE SPICE NOODLES

175 g (6 oz) plain flour

2 eggs

pinch of salt

½ tablespoon cumin seeds, toasted and ground

½ tablespoon coriander seeds, toasted and ground

½ tablespoon black peppercorns, toasted and ground

150 g (5 oz) fine semolina, for dusting

THE SAFFRON NOODLES

175 g (6 oz) plain flour

2 eggs

pinch of salt

1 level teaspoon saffron powder

150 g (5 oz) fine semolina, for dusting

Make the noodles in two separate batches using the same method for each.

Put the flour and eggs into a bowl and knead the spice or saffron mixture through it. Knead the dough ten times by passing it through the rollers of a pasta machine, folding the dough in half each time and dusting with semolina. Continue rolling down to the number one notch, then cut the dough into fine noodles. Put them under a damp cloth to rest.

Note: The spices need to be very finely ground or sieved, or else they will make holes in the thin sheets of pasta.

THE MACKEREL

4–6 fresh small mackerel, about 350 g (12 oz) each

200 g (7 oz) flour, seasoned with salt and pepper

25 ml (1 fl oz) olive oil

juice of 2–3 limes

2 bay leaves

freshly ground black pepper

50 g (2 oz) unsalted butter, cold and chopped

Fillet the mackerel and remove any small bones with tweezers, but leave the skin on. Lightly flour the skin side. Brush a heavy-based pan with a little oil. Heat until very hot, then sear the fish skin-side down. Sear the other side to seal. Transfer the fish fillets to a plate and keep warm.

Deglaze the pan with the lime juice and bring it to the boil, then add the bay leaves and black pepper. Whisk in the cold butter gradually and mix until it is all incorporated. Ladle this sauce over the fillets just before serving

Meanwhile, blanch the noodles for 30 seconds in boiling salted water and drain. Foam a knob or two of butter in a clean saute pan and toss the noodles until slightly browned. Serve the noodles with the fish fillets.

Picnics

Most food writers seem to agree that fresh air makes the very best of sauces. Almost as many romantic tales attach to the picnic as they do to the supper and at least one distinguished authority, the French philosopher of the kitchen, Jean Anthelme Brillat-Savarin, has suggested that they might, in their own small way, be as stimulating to passions other than appetite.

Brillat-Savarin has left a splendid account of the picnic in a piece written to celebrate the shooting luncheon. It begins as a quite straightforward outdoor meal with the hunter being captivated by a shady spot: "soft grass welcomes him, and the murmur of the nearby spring invites him to deposit in its cool waters the flask of wine destined to refresh him.

"Then with calm contentment, he takes out of his knapsack the cold chicken and golden-crusted rolls packed for him by loving hands, and places them beside the wedge of Gruyere or Roquefort which is to serve as his dessert." So far so good, but the writer doesn't leave the solitary hunter solitary for long and he goes on, "I have seen charming women and girls radiant with youth come gaily to the rendez-vous . . . I have seen them spread out on the grass turkey in transparent jelly, home made pâté, and salad ready for mixing; I have seen them dance light footed around the camp fire; I have taken part in the games and frolics which follow such gipsy meals, and I am convinced that they are not less gay, less charming, nor less pleasurable for want of luxury.

"And when the time comes to separate, why should not a few kisses be exchanged . . .?" Not quite the average barbie, perhaps, but Brillat-Savarin in that short description does distil the essence of the picnic and its simple elegance. Of course the reality might also involve mosquitoes and the ubiquitous Australian bush fly, sand in the sandwiches and wasps in the jam, but for all those small inconveniences, a meal eaten outdoors with the smell of wood smoke, is a very fine thing.

Picnics can go very wrong if a great deal of care is not taken in planning them. We once carefully hampered up what was left of a marvellous Christmas dinner—cold poached salmon, a side of smoked salmon, the remains of a rough stuffed roast goose, delicious cheeses and chilled champagne—and bravely blundered into an endless swamp. We were so unnerved by this misadventure that when we eventually emerged, battered and exhausted, onto solid ground an hour or two later, we only had the energy to drink the champagne, which by then was well and truly warmed and shaken. The food we pressed onto a pair of startled trampers who were about to lunch on a can of beans. No kisses followed that picnic.

The Victorians made the picnic into a grand formal occasion. The elaborate Victorian table was simply transferred to an outdoor setting with whole roasts of meat and fowl, cold game and potted meats, preserves and elaborate salads. The simple and delicious combinations hinted at by Brillat-Savarin were notable by their absence.

To a large extent Australia and New Zealand inherited that cumbersome Victorian tradition and it is only recently that we have borrowed from other cuisines for eating outdoors. Not the least of these imports being the barbecue, although that style is often debased by simply reducing it to burning steak and chops on an outdoor fire within feet of a perfectly good kitchen stove! All too often the whole Spanish-American cuisine of the barbecue is simply ignored in favour of what is only a rough cooking method designed to get mothers out of the kitchen and put fathers in charge.

The brasserie style is perfect for outdoor food. Many of the recipes in this book will translate to an outdoor version or could be prepared in advance to take on a picnic. Perhaps the essence of the picnic cuisine and that of the Bayswater Brasserie are almost identical—inventive and simple combinations of fresh ingredients. Elaboration, however much our Victorian ancestors were enamoured of it, has no place in the picnic repertoire. Sharp, fresh and surprising tastes do. Keep that in mind when choosing the liquid refreshments as well—Brillat-Savarin recommended white wine as ideal for the outdoor meal and it is hard to argue with that.

CHUTNEYS, PICKLES AND RELISHES

Chutneys, pickles and relishes ought to occupy the high ground in your picnic repertoire. An array of these, some fresh green salad leaves, crunchy bread, and cold cuts from the charcuterie, and you have a picnic. Not forgetting of course all those other ingredients essential to eating outdoors: a robust wine to wash it down with, congenial company and a pleasant view.

Don't forget either, that a picnic on a stormy day can be as wonderful in its own way as the more balmy kind. Pickles and chutneys, and especially a pungent relish are equally good fuel for those as well.

The ability to make these garnishes used to be an essential part of household skills. Sadly, the bottling and pickling days have gone from most urban Australian and New Zealand kitchens and there is, instead, a dangerous tendency to rely on the manufactured product. Not that there aren't some superb Asian and Indian condiments available—and many of them are made with techniques quite beyond the reach of the home cook.

As a general rule, chutneys, pickles and relishes will last for several weeks if stored in the refrigerator. If you wish to process them so they can be stored on the shelf for several months, refer to specialised books on the subject to ensure that you follow the processing method correctly.

If you accept the principal we offered earlier in the book, that the well stocked kitchen ought to be able to provide a satisfying lunch, then a few pickles, relishes and chutneys of your own are an essential store.

CHOKO AND PINEAPPLE CHUTNEY

MAKES 3 L (5 pts)

500 g (18 oz) chokos, peeled and chopped

5 medium-sized red Spanish onions, peeled and chopped

450 g (16 oz) pineapple, peeled, cored and chopped

475 g (17 oz) brown sugar

4 bay leaves

4 tablespoons black mustard seeds

4 tablespoons yellow mustard seeds

3 tablespoons turmeric powder

3 teaspoons sea salt

500 ml (18 fl oz) vinegar

Blanch the chokos in unsalted water, then drain and mix with all of the other ingredients. Bring to the boil and simmer for 30 minutes, skimming throughout cooking.

Note: If the chutney is not going to be stored in the fridge in a sealed jar, then it needs processing and storing on a shelf in a cool dark place.

TREE TOMATO CHUTNEY

About the same time as the Chinese gooseberry was transformed into the kiwi fruit, the humble tree tomato became the much more romantic tamarillo. The fruit is originally from South America and tamarillo may or may not be its original name.

Whatever its name, the tree tomato does equally well as a chutney or poached in a sweet syrup as a garnish to a pudding.

MAKES 3 L (5 pts)

700 g (1½ pts) tree tomatoes

3 medium-sized red Spanish onions, chopped

4 small sour apples, peeled, seeded and roughly chopped

250 g (9 oz) raisins

1 clove garlic

700 ml (1¼ pts) malt vinegar

200 g (7oz) brown sugar

1 tablespoon salt

pinch of cayenne pepper

1 teaspoon black mustard seeds

knob ginger root, peeled and chopped

1 cinnamon stick

pinch of dried chilli powder

Blanch the tree tomatoes in the same way as you would a tomato, and quarter them. Bring all the ingredients to the boil and simmer for 10–15 minutes. Store in a jar with a screw-top lid in the fridge, or pack and process into jars to store for a longer period on the shelf.

Note: If the chutney is not going to be stored in the fridge in a sealed jar, then it needs processing and storing on a shelf in a cool dark place.

PICKLED GREEN CHERRY TOMATOES

As Mrs Beaton might have said, first find your green tomatoes. You will probably need to talk your greengrocer or a grower into providing you with these unripe tomatoes.

MAKES 1½ L (2½ pts)

4 punnets of green cherry tomatoes

2 cloves garlic, peeled

½ teaspoon saffron threads

3 hot red chillies, seeded

2 fresh bay leaves

200 g (7 oz) sea salt

400 ml (14 fl oz) white wine vinegar

2½ L (4½ pts) water

1 tablespoon grated horseradish

Wash the tomatoes and remove any stems. Bring the rest of the ingredients to the boil and simmer until the salt has dissolved completely.

Pack the tomatoes into jars and pour the brine mixture over the top. Set aside for several weeks to pickle.

BREAD 'N' BUTTER PICKLES

This is a very simple pickle to make and is normally served on buttered bread. Like most simple things, though, it will not succeed unless you do it absolutely right. The vegetables must be crisp to the bite, so it is essential to salt them and let them stand for a few hours before pouring on the pickling liquid.

MAKES 3 L (5¼ pts)

THE VEGETABLES

125 g (4 oz) sea salt

1 dozen green bunching onions, green tops removed

2 red capsicums, seeds removed, cut into strips

2 green capsicums, seeds removed, cut into strips

½ head of cauliflower, in small florets

150 g (5 oz) flat green beans, strung and sliced diagonally

100 g (4 oz) snow peas

3 small Lebanese cucumbers

8 small yellow squash, quartered

2 garlic cloves, crushed

6 baby carrots, sliced into thin rounds

6 sticks celery, sliced

Salt all the vegetables, put them into a bucket and place 2 kg (4½ lb) ice over the top. Let them stand with the ice for 3 hours in the fridge.

THE SYRUP

1.1 kg (2½ lb) sugar

575 ml (20 fl oz) white wine vinegar

450 ml (16 fl oz) water

3 tablespoons sea salt

1½ tablespoons turmeric powder

1½ tablespoons mustard seeds

2 tablespoons celery seeds

3 hot red chillies, whole

Combine all of the syrup ingredients and bring them to the boil.

Drain the salted vegetables and pack them into a jar with a clip-locked lid with a rubber seal. Cover with the syrup and leave for 12 hours. They last about 3 weeks.

Note: The pickles can be processed in jars and stored for a longer period if you wish.

EGGPLANT AND OKRA RELISH

One of the pleasant features of this particular relish is the visual association of the baby eggplants and okra beans. The latter helps to thicken the relish to a nice consistency.

MAKES 3 L (5 pts)

450 g (16 oz) baby eggplants, split and salted
450 g (16 oz) baby okra beans, split
3 medium onions, chopped
800 ml (1½ pts) cider vinegar
300 g (11 oz) brown sugar
3 tablespoons ground allspice

1 tablespoon ground ginger
3 teaspoons sea salt
1 teaspoon ground black pepper
2 bay leaves
½ bunch fresh coriander, chopped

Bring all the ingredients, except the coriander, to the boil, and simmer for 10–15 minutes. Add the coriander. Bring back to the boil, then store in jars.

Note: If the relish is not going to be stored in a sealed jar in the fridge, then it needs processing and storing on a shelf in a cool dark place.

THELMA'S PLUM SAUCE

There is a famous sauce-making ancestor in almost every antipodean family and Thelma, my grandmother, holds this honoured position in mine. It is not an attribute confined to our culture alone however, and Madhur Jaffrey had a grandmother whose lime pickles were left as a much treasured inheritance to particularly important relatives.

MAKES 1 L (1¾ pts)

1.5 kg (3 lb 5 oz) blood plums, stoned
1 medium onion, peeled and roughly chopped
150 ml (5 fl oz) red wine vinegar
750 g (1½ lb) brown sugar

½ teaspoon cayenne pepper
1 teaspoon ground ginger
1 teaspoon sea salt

Bring all the ingredients to the boil. Simmer gently for about 3 hours, skimming throughout cooking. This should have the consistency of a tomato puree. Puree through the medium grill of a food mill or in a food processor.

Store in the fridge for 2 weeks before use. This can also be bottled and processed for longer storage.

SHREDDED SALT COD SALAD, PEAS AND ALMONDS

Salt cod is a very versatile preserved fish. For most dishes make sure that you soak it well, changing the water two or three times to restore the fish to respectability.

For this salad you can pull the fish apart and wash it to remove the salt. Rub it dry and into threads with a clean tea towel.

SERVES 6

100 g (4 oz) black-eyed beans, soaked overnight	*salt and pepper, to taste*
3 tablespoons olive oil	*400 g (14 oz) salt cod*
100 g (4 oz) blanched almonds	*curly endive, picked*
2 small onions, sliced	*½ bunch coriander leaves*
the juice of 1 lemon	*4 tablespoons Tree Tomato Chutney*
sherry vinegar	*(see page 168)*

Cook the beans in plenty of water for 1½ hours or until they are soft.

Heat the olive oil in a pan and fry the almonds until golden, drain and set aside, saving the oil. Mix together the remaining ingredients, except for the relish, and add the olive oil left over from the almonds. Serve the cod mixture on bread which has been spread with tomato relish.

COD AND POTATO CAKES

These cakes can be served either cold or warm. They can be made as small cakes and served on the side of a salad, or with meats and lashings of pickle or chutney. Make and pack them with care, since there is nothing quite so unappealing as a soggy fish cake that looks like someone has sat on it. That kind of caution applies to most picnic food. Its appeal is greatly enhanced if it arrives in the country or at the beach in kitchen-fresh condition.

SERVES 6–8

200 g (7 oz) salt cod, soaked overnight	*4 tablespoons port*
150 g (5 oz) potato, cooked and pureed through a food mill	*½ teaspoon ground pepper*
1 small onion, chopped	*2 eggs*
½ bunch parsley, chopped	*1 L (1²/₃ pts) grape seed oil, for frying*

Cook the cod for 20 minutes in plenty of water. Drain and remove all bones and skin. Put the flesh into a strong clean tea towel and bash it until the flesh is in threads. Make sure you use a *strong* tea towel or you will end up with bits of salt cod all over your kitchen.

Mix the cod with the potato, onion, parsley, port and pepper. Incorporate the eggs one at a time. Heat the oil in a high-sided pan to 180°C (350°F). Drop the cakes, which are formed with two spoons, into the oil, and cook until golden brown on all sides. Drain on absorbent paper.

COD AND PARSLEY BREAD

The dough used to make this bread is like the Portuguese version of brioche, which although it has some butter in it, is richer in olive oil. The bread is crisp and more robust than brioche. There is absolutely no point in turning a bread as wonderful as this into some exotic equivalent of a peanut butter or vegemite sandwich!

The Portuguese use strips of prosciutto as a common filling for their bread. We have suggested Borlotti Bean or Eggplant Puree as accompaniments to the Cod and Parsley Bread.

SERVES 6–8

THE DOUGH

250 g (9 oz) plain flour
15 g (½ oz) yeast

200 ml (7 fl oz) tepid water
¼ teaspoon salt
50 g (2 oz) butter

Sieve the flour into a bowl. Make a well in the centre and crumble the yeast into it. Add the tepid water and salt, and knead into a stiff dough. Add small amounts of the butter, a bit at a time, until it is all incorporated. Let this prove in a warm, draught-free place for 1 hour or until double in size.

THE FISH

300 g (11 oz) salt cod, soaked in water
   overnight
2 small Spanish onions, chopped

1 teaspoon freshly ground black pepper
½ bunch Italian parsley, picked and chopped
6 tablespoons olive oil

Cook the salt cod for 20 minutes in plenty of water to remove any excess salt. Flake the cod and discard any bones or skin. Mix the cod with the onions, pepper, parsley and half the olive oil. Let this marinate for about 15 minutes.

Push two thirds of the dough into an 18 x 23 cm (7 x 9 in) pie dish, dipping your fingers into the remaining olive oil if they are sticking. Cover the dough with the salt cod mixture, leaving 3 cm (1¼ in) around the edges. Fold the edges up over the cod and begin stretching the remaining third of the dough over the top, making sure this goes over the top of the dough edges. Sprinkle more of the olive oil over the dough and press it down so that it is quite flat. Do not prove any further. Bake the bread immediately for 25 minutes in an oven preheated to 200°C (400°F).

SPANISH MACKEREL CUTLETS AND BROCCOLI FLOWERS

In Europe a dish like this is presented with the tender flowers from the top of the Galician cabbage, but the tiny yellow flowers from Chinese broccoli are a perfect substitute. If you cannot find the Chinese species, use regular broccoli, leaving the flower heads on long thin stalks.

Assemble this dish as a complete meal, packed tightly into its serving dish, before you leave home.

SERVES 4

THE CUTLETS AND SALAD

4 x 175 g (6 oz) Spanish mackerel cutlets
200 ml (7 fl oz) Fish Stock (see page 23)
1 bay leaf
2 medium onions
2 tablespoons olive oil
4 tomatoes, peeled, seeded and chopped
2 teaspoons paprika

4 tablespoons red wine vinegar
salt and pepper, to taste
a 10 cm (4 in) piece stale French bread
4 small Pontiac potatoes, boiled and halved
4 hard-boiled eggs, peeled and halved
1 tablespoon tiny salted capers, washed
2 bunches Chinese broccoli, blanched

Put the fish into the cold stock with the bay leaf and bring it to the boil. Simmer for 3–4 minutes, then set aside to cool.

Saute the onions in olive oil until golden brown, add the tomatoes and paprika. Deglaze the pan with the vinegar and season with salt and pepper. Break the bread into the sauce, then cook until reduced and thick. This will take about 5 minutes.

Arrange the potatoes, cutlets, eggs and capers on the broccoli and pour the sauce over the top. Serve this with crunchy French bread.

BORLOTTI BEAN AND EGGPLANT PUREES

Purees are as essential for picnic garnishes as are the more common pickles and chutneys, although they do not enjoy the recognition that they richly deserve. You can serve them as a garnish or with wedges of interesting bread, or they can be used to cheer up the Great Australian Sandwich—and not before time either.

BORLOTTI BEAN PUREE
750 g (1½ lb) fresh borlotti beans

1 L (1²/₃ pts) Chicken Stock (see page 23)
salt and pepper, to taste

Cook the beans in the stock for 40 minutes or until they are soft. Puree with the stock and season with salt and pepper.

EGGPLANT PUREE
4 medium eggplants
2 tablespoons capers

1 red capsicum, grilled and peeled
salt and pepper, to taste

Roast the eggplants in an oven preheated to 200°C (400°F) for 25 minutes or until soft. Remove them from the oven and puree to a smooth paste in a food processor with the rest of the ingredients.
Serve either of these purees with wedges of Cod and Parsley Bread.

ROAST POTATO TART WITH BEETROOT AND MACHE SALAD

The combination of beetroot and mache in a salad is often served in French brasseries.
If your approach to meals is traditional Australian or New Zealand, then this picnic dish is ideal for long weekends. You can use the left over roast potatoes from the Sunday roast dinner for Monday's picnic. Slice them up, bake them in a tart and serve them with some of the cold roast meat and a vigorous pickle.

SERVES 8–10
THE TART
300 g (11 oz) puff pastry
1 tablespoon butter
1 medium onion, chopped
½ bunch spring onions

3 medium tomatoes, peeled, seeded and chopped
8 medium potatoes, roasted
4 eggs
salt and pepper
150 mls (5 fl oz) cream

Line a 30 cm (12 in) flan tin with the pastry and bake blind (see page 35). Heat the butter in a medium-sized pan and saute the onion until it is transparent. Mix in the spring onions and tomatoes, then spread the mixture over the bottom of the pastry case. Overlap the sliced potatoes on top of the mixture.

Beat the eggs, salt, pepper and cream together without whisking too much air into the mixture, then pour it into the tart. Bake the tart in an oven preheated to 180°C (350°F) for 45 minutes.

THE SALAD
4 tablespoons olive oil
2 tablespoons raspberry vinegar
2 sprigs of fresh rosemary

salt and pepper
3 dozen small bunches mache leaves
3 dozen baby beetroots, cooked (see page 88)

Whisk the olive oil into the vinegar. Add the rosemary, and season. Toss the mache leaves and beetroots in the rosemary dressing. Serve the salad with the tart.

HOT SMOKED QUAILS WITH SMASHED CUCUMBER SALAD

When I was 17 years old, I tried smoking several eels. Unfortunately the 44-gallon drum was still hot when the fish went in and they cooked before they were smoked. The eels had been split open and threaded on wires. As they cooked, the wires pulled their heads off and they fell into the hot coals, ending up charred through, though still quite delicious to eat.

The next time I encountered smoking was while working in Amsterdam. This time it was a much smaller and simpler production, and the result was not in the least burned. We would use a small box with special wood chips from Scandinavia in the bottom. A single-portion sized piece of Scotch salmon was set on the rack and the fish was hot-smoked in about 10 minutes over a bare flame. This was usually served with a lemon beurre blanc, as beurre blanc was the popular accompaniment in those days.

Since then I have smoked foods in the oven using various dried herbs and brown sugar, and had quite a lot of success. If you have a fire or a barbecue it is very easy, while picnicking, to hot-smoke your lunch. Certain fishing shops sell small smoking boxes and wood chips are available from barbecue shops, although good, dry, vine trimmings are a favourite.

SERVES 6

THE QUAILS AND MARINADE

12 large quails, spatchcocked (see page 114)

zest and juice of 3 lemons

3 tablespoons walnut oil

3 cloves garlic, peeled and smashed

½ teaspoon freshly ground black pepper

Mix all the ingredients together and marinate the quails for 3 hours before the picnic.

THE SALAD

2 cloves garlic, peeled and crushed

1 x 200 g (7 oz) piece daikon radish, peeled and finely sliced

400 ml (14 fl oz) rice vinegar

200 ml (7 fl oz) light soy sauce

125 ml (4 fl oz) sesame oil

600 ml (1 pt) water

6 small Lebanese cucumbers, topped and tailed

Combine the garlic and daikon with the vinegar, soy, oil and water. Gently smash the cucumbers with the flat of a large splitting knife or chopper, slicing up the larger pieces. Put the cucumber in the marinade and set aside.

To hot-smoke the quail, put a reasonable amount of chips in the bottom of the box and place it over hot coals. Let the quails cook for 10 minutes, then serve with the salad.

COLD ROAST VEAL NUT WITH BREAD 'N' BUTTER PICKLES

This veal nut, studded with anchovies, thin slivers of garlic and sprigs of marjoram, is a wonderful cold meat. Roast meats look better when they have just been sliced, so take this whole to the picnic spot and slice it there. Obviously you will need to pack a very sharp knife—the only thing worse than leaving that behind is forgetting the corkscrew.

We serve the meat with pickles and sauce, but it is equally acceptable in a sandwich.

Next to the pie, pizza or calzoni, the English sandwich is one of the world's great portable meals. Its invention is attributed to a dissolute eighteenth century Lord Sandwich, who was too obsessed to leave the gaming table for a meal and dined on a slice of meat between two slices of bread. From those humble beginnings have come great wonders.

It is, in fact, hard to accept this popular account, as universal as it is. Before plates became fashionable, food was served on slices of stale bread called trenchers (hence the description of one who enjoys a hearty meal as a trencherman or, as we would have it now, trencherperson) and that would seem a logical first step to the sandwich. So too would the peasant workaday lunch of a lump of bread with cheese and pickles.

Part of the sandwich's history includes a hunter's version, where the bread is toasted on one side—the outside—to reduce its propensity to crumble in the pocket. This treatment is worth a revival as a means of retaining some of the bread's crispness against a moist filling.

SERVES 4–6

THE VEAL NUT

1 x 900 g (2 lb) nut of veal

10 large anchovy fillets, rinsed

5 cloves garlic, peeled and thinly sliced

1 small bunch marjoram, picked

salt and pepper, to taste

100 ml (3½ fl oz) olive oil

1 small onion, peeled and chopped

1 medium carrot, peeled and chopped

1 head celeriac, peeled and chopped

Trim the veal of all sinew. Push a short, sharp knife into it to make 3 cm (1 in) incisions over the joint. Push the anchovies, garlic and marjoram into the holes and season with salt and pepper.

Heat the oil in a pan and seal the veal. Place it on a bed of the chopped vegetables in an oven preheated to 220°C (425°F) for 10 minutes, then roast it for a further 10 minutes at 180°C (360°F). Remove the veal from the oven and let it cool.

Slice the veal before the picnic or take a sharp knife and slice it on the spot. Roast meats look better when they have just been sliced unless they have been well chilled. Serve the meat slices brushed with a little plum sauce and a pile of bread 'n' butter pickles, and, of course, bread.

Note: Anchovies are best when they are stored whole in salt. Obviously these are more work since they need to be washed and filletted, but the effort is worth it for the quality of the fish in this form.

TRIPE TERRINE

This is a jellied terrine as opposed to a baked meaty loaf. Tripe is available already blanched by the butcher. In fact it is very hard to find uncooked tripe. It is best used with strong flavours, like tomato, vinegar and red wine for example. The classic dish, Tripe Lyonnaise, is a sort of sticky dish with onions and tomato paste, which are a perfect match with the strong flavour of the tripe.

In this case, the tripe is set in a sharp jelly with sweetbreads, dried tomatoes, olives and other diced vegetables. It can be served with many other garnishes, such as roast tomatoes, sweet and sour leeks, red capsicum salad with raisin and onion relish, and so on.

The basic idea of this dish, using a jelly to hold the garnish, is one you can experiment with.

SERVES 8–10

THE JELLIED STOCK

6 pig's trotters, soaked overnight in salted water

1 large leek, roughly chopped

3 medium onions, roughly chopped

2 medium carrots, roughly chopped

10 cracked black peppercorns

4 fresh bay leaves

a couple of sprigs of thyme

2 cloves garlic, chopped

juice of 1 lemon

150 ml (5 fl oz) white wine vinegar

3 L (5¼ pts) Chicken Stock (see page 23)

In a deep pan, cover all the ingredients with the chicken stock. Bring to the boil and skim thoroughly. Simmer for 4 hours, skimming and maintaining the liquid at all times. Strain off the stock and discard the vegetables and trotters. Reduce the stock to 1.5 L (2½ pts) and reserve.

THE TRIPE AND GARNISH

1 kg (2 lb 3 oz) tripe, cooked

4 medium pickled pork hocks

2 small carrots, sliced

1 medium leek, peeled and chopped

1 medium head of celeriac, peeled and chopped

dried tomatoes, drained and dried

300 g (11 oz) sweetbreads, cooked (see page 95)

½ bunch parsley, chopped

2 bunches chervil, chopped

150 g (5 oz) Pickled Green Cherry Tomatoes (see page 168)

Cook the tripe in the reserved stock for 15 minutes. Remove and roll it in a clean tea towel, then cool in the fridge. Cool the reserved stock.

Simmer the pork hocks in enough water to cover for 2 hours, or until they are tender and the meat is falling off the bone.

Meanwhile, poach the vegetables, including the dried tomatoes, until they are cooked through. Cool and drain the vegetables and carefully mix together with the cooked hocks, sweetbreads and chopped herbs. Cut the tripe into 5 mm (¼ in) strips and mix through the vegetable mixture. Assemble the ingredients in a crockery terrine mould and cover with the cool stock. Set in the fridge, preferably overnight. Serve with a small pile of the cherry tomatoes and some crunchy bread.

INDEX OF RECIPES

INDEX